Self Harm

Why Teens Do It And What Parents Can Do To Help

Michelle Mitchell

16pt

Copyright Page from the Original Book

Note: The information contained in this book should not substitute medical and/or professional advice, or personal judgement. The author and publisher accept no responsibility for any action taken as a result of this material. Names have been changed or omitted to protect privacy at the request of schools and parents.

Copyright © Michelle Mitchell

First published 2019

Copyright remains the property of the author and apart from any fair dealing for the purposes of private study, research, criticism or review, as permitted under the Copyright Act, no part may be reproduced by any process without written permission.

All inquiries should be made to the publishers.

Big Sky Publishing Pty Ltd
PO Box 303, Newport, NSW 2106, Australia
Phone: 1300 364 611
Fax: (61 2) 9918 2396
Email: info@bigskypublishing.com.au
Web: www.bigskypublishing.com.au

Cover design and typesetting: Think Productions
Printed in China by Hang Tai Printing Company Limited

For Cataloguing-in-Publication entry see National Library of Australia.

Author: Michelle Mitchell

Title: Self Harm; Why teens do it and what parents can do to help

TABLE OF CONTENTS

Endorsements	i
A Quick Definition	viii
Why I Wrote This Book	ix
1: The Important Basics	1
2: The Psychology and Physiology	28
3: The Role of the Internet	51
4: Digital Self-Harm	79
5: Must-Have Conversations	122
6: The Role of Professional Support and Schools	155
7: Self-Care and Safety Plans	183
8: Parent as Coach	212
9: Taking Care of Family	236
10: Stories of Hope	251
Acknowledgements	283
Resources and Websites	288
About the Author	293
Endnotes	295
Reference List	313
Back Cover Material	324

Endorsements

Michelle Mitchell's book SELF HARM is a valuable exploration of one of the most misunderstood and frightening behaviours that occurs for many young people on their adolescent journey. Michelle's wisdom, warmth and compassion mirror what is really needed for those who are supporting a young person who is self-harming. This is a must for families, schools and community organisations that work with young people. Together we can all make a positive difference with really accurate knowledge and understanding that is found is this excellent book.

Maggie Dent – author, educator and parents and resilience specialist

Parents are often frightened and overwhelmed when they discover their child is self-harming. It is an issue that is not spoken about enough. This book is packed with research, expert advice and very brave personal stories, which will provide many parents with support and hope. Michelle has done an incredible job in addressing a very sensitive topic.

Collett Smart – psychologist, educator and author

With compelling wisdom and compassion, Michelle Mitchell has lifted the curtain on self-harm. She draws on important research and extensive experience and provides vivid examples that are so raw and so ordinary in their truth, as to give a strong and poignant voice, not only to those who are self-harming, but also to the ones who love them. This book traverses that gap. It is an intelligent, thoughtful, and much-needed resource, empowering all who read it with powerful insights, a road map of practical strategies, and above all else, hope.

Karen Young – author, speaker, parenting and child & adolescent anxiety specialist

This is a practical, compassionate, best-practice book that is accessible to any parent. Michelle combines understanding with genuine care to help

any family with teens who struggle. I read every word! Highly recommended!
Dr Justin Coulson – bestselling author and one of Australia's leading parenting experts

This book is a much needed resource for any parent, carer or educator that is dealing with a young person in the grips of self-harm. This resource is incredibly timely and not only provides sound and well researched guidance, but also hope and a way forward.
Sharon Witt – bestselling author, educator and presenter

Delegates at the Resilient Kids Conference were inspired and encouraged sitting under Michelle's teaching. Her relational style combined with her depth of wisdom and experience connects the room powerfully. Michelle tackles a difficult discussion with an intentionally inclusive and equipping voice. Michelle is a true power-house on her topic, yet with an engaging and gentle heart.

Janet Nyhouse – Resilient Kids Conference event manager

Reading Michelle's excellent approach to this challenging subject of 'Self Harming,' has given me a much greater awareness and understanding of this issue, and I feel better equipped to help individuals and families thus affected. At times it was disturbing and painful to read, but Michelle has ensured there is hope strewn throughout the pages. This book will empower parents, teachers, laypeople and professionals as they help navigate children through the challenges of self-harm.

Pastor Anne Luliano-founder of Chaplaincy Australia and NSW Ambulance chaplain, chaplaincy trainer

Reading this has left me heartbroken that self-harm is so prevalent among young Australians. Encouraged, that there are experts like Michelle who have hearts, minds and shoulders big enough to carry the burden of working in this space, and hopeful that we, as parents, can be equipped to help our children navigate the darkness of self-harm to a more bright and healthy future.

Katie Hotko (mother of three)

When Michelle broached the subject of writing a book about self-harming I was jumping up & down with joy – finally someone brave enough to tackle the confronting topic, one that has impacted our family, and countless others; a topic that is so often misunderstood; a topic that we often don't want to talk about, not in public anyway. Whether you read her books or have the privilege of hearing her speak, you will walk away with tools relevant to living a more positive life, and the biggest gift of all – hope.

Melinda Paulo (mother of two)

SELF HARM should be required reading for every parent with children. Michelle Mitchell presents facts and figures, personal stories from families of self-harmers and most importantly, she gives adults the tools and resources necessary to handle this issue, including behaviors that could be a signal of self-harm, how to compassionately approach the subject with the young

person and the differences between females and males who self-harm.
Michelle Koe Page, PharmD Mom, pharmacist, consultant and co-founder of Unbreakable Moms

I highly recommend that every parent, carer, guardian, teacher, youth worker, chaplain and counsellor read Michelle's new book *Self-harm*. It will give the insight, empathy, understanding and tools you need to walk alongside young people and families who are facing self-harm. Michelle's non-judgmental and comprehensive approach to unpacking this issue from a variety of different angles is incredibly helpful in appreciating how we can all play a role in understanding and helping young people with this. A must read. Thank you Michelle.
Lousie Klar – student counsellor, Genesis Christian College

This book is dedicated to every parent whose young person is self-harming, with special thoughts going to those whom I have had the privilege of supporting over the past twenty years.

I pray that our sons and daughters grow strong and courageous in the face of adversity and pain, and that we continue to believe that happiness is possible for each human being.

A Quick Definition

Non-suicidal self-injury (NSSI) is defined as deliberately injuring oneself without suicidal intent or ideation. People who deliberately injure themselves do so in an attempt to cope with, express or control emotional pain. NSSI is a global mental health concern, with the majority of people who self-harm aged between 11 and 25 years old. Throughout the book NSSI will be referred to simply as self-harm.

Why I Wrote This Book

Twenty years ago, I left my teaching position and founded Youth Excel, a charity that delivered life skills education, mentoring and psychological services to thousands of young people and their families. It led me into all areas of the health and wellbeing sector, working alongside the most marvellous guidance officers, psychologists, doctors and specialists. My career has been a very grassroots and hands-on one.

One of the highlights was establishing The Youth Excel Centre, a multidisciplinary clinic that offered psychology, counselling and mentoring services to approximately 120 families each week. These services were provided from our offices and onsite at schools throughout Brisbane, Australia. We dealt with a lot of incidents of self-harm involving both males and females, from primary age all the way up to young adults ... and occasionally their parents.

As the research suggests, treating self-harm can be challenging. This often leads parents to look for alternative methods of support. Perhaps that is why parents regularly rang the Youth Excel Centre, asking me to mentor their teens. These young people were either refusing to see a psychologist or wanting to visit a mentor in conjunction with a psychologist. Some young people perceived a mentor as less threatening or clinical. Some medical professionals directly referred to me as they felt a mentor was a good fit for young people who had been 'around all services and back again'. I always suggest young people see a medical professional in conjunction with any nonmedical support.

Looking back over my journey, I can honestly say that some of my most memorable 'career moments' have been with young people who have overcome the desire to self-harm. Eunice, whom I had the privilege of mentoring during her high school years, now accompanies me to some of my presentations to parents and professionals about self-harm. You will find her story in

Chapter 10. Today she studies psychology at university, but I remember the days when her mother literally mopped pools of blood from the bathroom floor and confiscated razors that seemed to be breeding in her room. Those were days that no mother would want to repeat.

I have seen the absolute helplessness in parents' eyes when they are faced with the brutal reality that they can't control their children's feelings or behaviour. There is nothing more agonising for parents than to see cuts on their daughter's thighs, or bruises or burns on their son's arms, knowing that the behaviour was deliberate and likely to be repeated. It takes immense courage and strength to walk beside your children during their most challenging times. Time and time again I hear young people who have overcome self-harm praise their mums and dads for standing with and for them.

As I wrote this book I interviewed young people, parents, educators and psychologists. They all agreed that parents are in the 'hot seat' of significance in their child's life and have a great impact on a self-harming child's trajectory.

I therefore cannot empower and support parents enough as they guide young minds to stay calm, cope well and live their best lives.

If you have a child who is struggling with self-harm, I want to remind you that *you* are your child's greatest advantage. The psychologist you are paying will add value, but can't replace *you*. The chaplain at the school that you have invested so much hope into will add value, but can't replace you either. *You* are uniquely graced to parent your children and you are irreplaceable in their lives. *You* are their constant. Your connection with them is everything in their self-discovery and recovery.

I often say that parenting is usually difficult when you are doing a good job of it. This is especially true when parenting a young person who is struggling with self-harm. There is no doubt that self-harm will test every ounce of patience, strength and courage that a parent can muster. There is also no doubt that a loving parent somehow finds all these attributes and more when they are required.

Although self-harm is a confronting topic, it is one which is incredibly important to shed light on. I believe that through more honest and open discussion we can break the silence that surrounds this significant health concern. These pages contain critical information to help parents prevent, understand or respond to self-harm.

I have found that once we are armed with practical tools for today, tomorrow is always easier.

1

The Important Basics

Self-harm is one of those topics that remains very difficult for many adults to understand. 'Why would anyone want to harm themselves?' is the question on most adults' minds. 'Why would MY child want to harm themselves?' is the question that parents whose children are self-harming wrestle with on a daily basis.

Self-harm seems to go against every innate instinct of self-protection and survival. It is therefore a confusing and distressing concept for parents, grandparents, siblings and friends to come to terms with. It can evoke the strongest feelings of anxiety. Family members can naturally become highly protective and reactive, and live in an unhealthy and exhausting state of high alert.

It is also not uncommon for me to hear tones of frustration from teachers as they talk about self-harm. They might say, 'She's just ruining her body',

'Maybe he just needs to toughen up', 'Everyone has issues. What makes her life so dramatic?' or, 'I wonder how much of this is just about attention?'

I notice that professionals' default reaction is often shaming, blaming and criticising – not because they don't want to help, but because they don't know how else to handle it.

I have even secretly found myself thinking, 'What can possibly be this bad?' when faced with a client I was unable to make progress with. It can feel very frustrating when you want the best for someone who doesn't want the best for themselves. However, to 'get it' I have had to make a conscious effort. I have had to personally approach each young person struggling with self-harm with an open heart and patience.

A Definition

The official term for self-harm is non-suicidal self-injury (NSSI), which simply means deliberately injuring yourself without suicidal intent or ideation.

Most young people deliberately injure themselves in an attempt to cope with, express or control emotional pain. Some use self-harm as a form of self-punishment. Although self-harm may bring temporary relief it is important to note that it does not solve problems.

The 2015 Mental Health Child and Adolescent Report tells us that approximately 10% of young people consciously experiment with self-harm at some stage through high school. Other research estimates self-harm ranges between 7 and 24%, with initiation in the middle school years. Self-harm is probably a lot more common than most research suggests, as surveys are usually conducted with young people who go to hospital or their GP after self-harming. We know that a lot of young people do not seek help after they self-harm and that behaviour is often hidden from clinical services.

Although some very young children and some adults are known to self-harm and it can continue from childhood into adulthood, the majority of people who self-harm are aged between 11 and 25 years. Those who self-harm more than once usually cease this behaviour within two years, and only 20% persist for more than five years. It is not uncommon for young people to grow out of self-harm and develop other coping strategies as they move through their teenage years into adulthood.

However, it is also recognised that a history of self-harm is the greatest predictor of recurrent behaviour in adulthood. Since one in three young people who self-harm will do it again in the following year, self-harm can be classed as highly addictive behaviour.

I am particularly passionate about the early intervention and prevention of self-harm because during this time it is most responsive to the support that caring adults can bring.

The Link to Suicide

When parents find out that their son or daughter is self-harming they often question whether their young person wants to die. For this reason, I want to give this topic some specific discussion and hope to answer some of your questions in an honest, balanced and thought-provoking way.

Self-harm can be performed with the intention to die (attempted suicide) or without the intention to die. Rates for non-suicidal self-harm are up to three times higher than self-harm with suicidal intent, although it is acknowledged that it is difficult to clearly separate intent from behaviour.

It was previously thought that self-harm existed on a continuum of severity with suicidal behaviour. However, today self-harm is increasingly recognised as an important health issue in its own right, with a psychology of its own. Although the link between suicide and self-harm definitely needs to be researched further, there is enough evidence to suggest that self-harm can stand completely independent of suicidal thoughts or actions. It is important for us to understand that people who self-harm do not necessarily want to die.

I have personally been involved with hundreds of young people who have self-harmed and had no intention of suicide. Some have talked about wanting to die, but their real motive was wanting to escape their current situation rather than wanting to end their life. I have also been involved with a few young people who *did* attempt suicide. Some of those attempts were 'out of the blue' – with no discussion of suicide prior to their attempt – and others were anticipated. All were heart-wrenching and tragic for their families and me.

Shae's Story

Shae came to see me after at least a year of regular self-harm. The 15-year-old was struggling with significant depression. Shae was also questioning her sexuality. These were significant things for her to deal with in addition to all the so-called 'normal' dramas of high school.

Shae was willing for her mother to share her story in this book to help other families understand self-harm in a better way. I honour her family for their courage. As I read her words, it was reiterated to me how deeply parents feel their children's pain. I hope this speaks to you in some way and Shae's journey provides families going through a tough time with hope.

Here is her story through her mother's eyes:

Our eldest daughter cut to feel numb. The cutting gave her pain – pain which she felt she deserved. She cut secretly. She cut and kept it very well hidden, cutting her upper thighs. She had found a pocket knife which she kept in her room. Our girl kept it all very close. We had no idea. Often, she'd withdraw, not wanting any sort of contact. I would simply lie next to her on her bed; often she didn't want to be touched, but my mumma's heart just wanted to wrap her up and take away all the pain!

We took her to a GP and they did all the usual tests like bloods and checks to start with. They wanted to check whether there was anything physical causing her moods. There was nothing physically wrong except low iron. They suggested we find a psychologist.

She was already seeing the school counsellor. It was in this process that it came out that she was struggling with her sexuality. That was really difficult for us as a family but we were determined to find the right person for us and for her.

When everything came out in the open she was overwhelmed. She attempted a drug overdose, wanting simply to go to sleep, to not have to deal with anything anymore, tired of feeling nothing. We couldn't believe it. I held it all together, calling paramedics, dealing with the ride to the hospital, the stay overnight and the millions of questions ... until we got her safely back home and tucked back into her own bed.

Then I sat in the bottom of the shower and sobbed. I wanted to scream and shout and hurt someone. I understood a little of what my teenager was feeling. This was our darkest time. As a parent I felt totally isolated. There was the fear of being judged. The feeling that I had failed or was failing her. It was the whole grief cycle and it is amazing how quickly you can spin through it. I felt so alone.

At times I wanted to stand on the doorstep and yell out, 'I need help' and then other times I wanted to shut the door because I felt so vulnerable.

For our girl, there were other deep issues that came to the surface during this time and again we reached out for professional help. Finding the right person for Shae to see was everything. We didn't want someone imposing their thoughts on our daughter and we wanted someone who would work with our whole family and not exclude us as parents. We wanted her to find someone that she felt safe with too. That took a while for us to find.

During this time we organised a mini room makeover, framing positive quotes. We made a lot of progress together as a family. Looking back now it was a good time for us all. We are proud to say that our girl graduated Year 12 – 'touch & go' for a while there, but we made it! Getting ready for the formal was transforming for her. To see in the mirror that she is beautiful broke the label or box she had put herself in. I kept saying to her, 'Now you see what I see every day!'

She's now working part time. She hasn't got a firm direction for the future, but we aren't as worried about that. She's alive, she laughs, she smiles, she's happy! I want to say to any family in the middle of a difficult time that there is hope.

Will she always smile? I don't know. Will she ever cut again? I don't know. But if we got through it once I know we can get through it again, and she is older and more mature now. I feel we would do so much better if it were to ever resurface.

One of the things is that we have a promise between us now – that we will talk.

Particularly after her graduation, there were a few bumps that we came across ... and we came back to our promise: we will talk.

Later, I saw Shae and her mother at an event I spoke at. I had to do a double take, because Shae was unrecognisable compared to the girl I met many years ago. She was strong, smiling, purposeful and enjoying good relationships. We met with hugs and more hugs! You can't celebrate life enough! I reminded myself once again that there is hope for every child going through a dark time.

Although the focus of this book is non-suicidal self-harm, you will notice that some of the stories featured do reveal suicidal intent or ideation. I hope this depicts the complexity of self-harm, and the reality that self-harm may be intertwined with suicide. If you are ever concerned about a young person's suicidal tendencies, the obvious advice is to visit a doctor or hospital or call an ambulance immediately.

It is too easy to become familiar with our own children and draw inaccurate conclusions, so an objective opinion is important.

A doctor will conduct a suicide risk assessment and provide you with a management plan and referrals to specialists. This management plan may include common sense precautions like removing sharp objects, prescription medication and other high-risk household items. If necessary, they may admit a young person to hospital.

Who is Susceptible

To many people's surprise, self-harm is not classified as a mental health disorder. It is, however, highly possible that a young person has a mental health disorder at the time that they self-harm. Anxiety, depression, and impulsivity are often key factors, although it will take an assessment by a mental health professional to determine their contribution.

It takes an open mind for parents to look past self-harm behaviour and towards their young person's general wellbeing, especially if a young person's mental health has seemed stable in the past. Self-harm can often come 'out of the blue' for parents, and I have found some parents do not want to consider the link between self-harm and the perceived label of 'mental illness'. Some parents may fear the instant progression to medication or psychological treatment, when they do not feel it is warranted.

As mum of 15-year-old Amy explained:

> The biggest discovery during this journey for both Amy and me was the severe anxiety Amy was suffering. We had no idea that she was struggling with anxiety before this came out. It sounds ridiculous to say that now, almost embarrassing, but we just never saw it. It took me a while to come to terms with the fact that my daughter was struggling with something greater than self-harm. The anxiety was taking away Amy's ability to process her thoughts and emotions. Awareness of the feelings of anxiety, and how to deal with them before it rose any further has allowed Amy to take control back.

Poor mental health plus stressful life events (including family issues or personal pain) make young people more susceptible to self-harm. It is the combination of elements which becomes overwhelming for young people and often leads them to poor coping mechanisms. Increased frequency and severity of self-harm is associated with an increased combination of these elements. A family history of mental illness is also a key risk factor.

Self-harm has been linked to trauma and distress. In my work with young people I have found these to be some of the recurring issues associated with self-harm:

- poor relationships with friends
- bullying and/or cyberbullying
- family separation or conflict at home
- perfectionism or pressure be a high achiever
- gay, lesbian, bisexual or transgender sexual orientation
- abuse, especially sexual abuse
- poverty or low income
- poor academic performance
- serious illness of family or friends
- poor parent–child attachment
- suicide or self-harm of others

- low self-esteem, particularly associated with body image
- eating disorders
- poor mental health and/or family history of poor mental health

The Warning Signs

It is common for parents to feel shocked when they discover their young person has been self-harming. I often remind parents that they don't see what they aren't looking for. It is so easy for parents to miss the warning signs of self-harm, especially because self-harm is usually a personal experience, entrenched in secrecy and shame. Parents may know that 'something isn't right' but they may not notice or see direct evidence of self-harm for some time after it has begun.

It is easy for parents to miss the warning signs. One father I interviewed said, 'I saw cuts on her leg and she told me she had fallen over on sharp grass during PE. I actually believed her at the time. I didn't think about it anymore until I saw cuts on her arm. That is when it clicked. That was at least two years ago now. Looking back, I wish I had been more aware and addressed things earlier.'

Some of the common warning signs of self-harm include:
- knowledge of others who are self-harming
- unexplained marks on body
- wearing long sleeves that are never removed
- covering up or wearing baggy clothing
- wearing wide wrist bands that are never removed
- secretive behaviour
- items that could be used for cutting going missing or put in strange places (like the back of drawers)
- needing to be alone for long periods of time
- physical or social isolation
- blood stains
- sharp objects found amongst possessions
- frequent stories of accidents
- sleeping and eating changes
- losing interest in usual pleasures
- mood changes

- avoiding situations where arms and legs are showing eg. gymnastics or swimming carnival
- washing their own clothes
- drop in grades at school

Types of Self-Harm

The ways in which young people self-harm are wide and varied. Simply google 'creative ways to self-harm' and you will find out how wide and varied they actually are. Although people may think of self-harm as cutting, some of the less recognised methods include electrocution, burning, self-battery, jumping from dangerous heights, stopping medication suddenly, pulling hair, needle sticking, freezing, strangling, suffocating, overdosing, swallowing a non-ingestible object, train surfing, driving at high speeds and deliberate unsafe sex. A newer form of self-harm is digital self-harm, which I will discuss in Chapter 4.

I have seen both males and females hold their breath until they pass out, smash fingertips with a hammer or in a car door, scratch wounds so they won't heal, insert lead from pencils under their skin, burn their skin with lighters or hot water, swallow poisonous substances, jump from heights that they know aren't safe, and deliberately bash their limbs against walls so that they break bones.

I would also like to point out that it is the *intention* of the behaviour that classifies self-harm, rather than the behaviour itself.

For example, young people who binge drink may do so for a lot of reasons. They may do so to have fun or gain social status, or to self-harm—or for a combination of these reasons.

Some years back I noticed it was popular for girls to carry a self-harm kit in their school bag, filled with blades, bobby pins, broken compasses, pencils and knives just in case they had the urge to self-harm. In some schools, girls would carry their kits to group self-harm sessions. Group self-harm sessions are a rarer platform for self-harm. Online self-harm sessions are similar to group self-harm sessions but may have anonymity, depending on their nature.

Parents often ask me if eating disorders are a form of self-harm. Eating disorders are officially classified as a mental disorder in their own right, with the core intention to change a person's appearance rather than cause harm. However, eating disorders are seldom independent behaviours and are commonly linked to other destructive coping strategies, including self-harm. It is possible for young people to use eating disorder symptoms such as induced vomiting or excessive exercise to self-harm. Again, intention classifies self-harm.

Research from *The Place of Self-Harm in Adolescent Development* puts self-harm into the following categories: cutting (55.9%), overdosing (22%), self-battery (11%) and other multiple methods (10%). This explains why self-harm is often called 'cutting'. The multiple methods category is a miscellaneous category which groups together any other form of self-harm that is not defined as cutting, overdosing or self-battery.

Gender Differences

I would like to share my experiences with how gender interacts with self-harm, in a hope to broaden your understanding and ability to communicate with young people. Although I am aware there will be many exceptions to these thoughts, I know these views will support some readers.

Most studies suggest females participate in self-harm at higher rates than males. *The Child and Adolescent Self-Harm in Europe (CASE) Study*, which surveyed over 30,000 mainly fifteen and sixteen-year-olds, suggests approximately 8% of females as opposed to 5% of males deliberately self-harm. The *Self-Harm and Suicide in Adolescents* research paper specifically comments on the differences between boys and girls 12 to 15 years old, noting that the ratio is as high as five or six to one.

Research certainly suggests strong differences between male and female self-harming tendencies, with males leaning towards high-risk behaviour and girls tending towards self-injury. Females were more likely to report self-cutting and overdosing but were less likely to use methods such as self-battery, hanging or jumping.

Very few young men who I interviewed for this book were willing to publicly share their experiences with self-harm. They were also hesitant to admit to self-harm because they saw it as a 'female issue'. In my experience, boys are far less likely to identify self-harm as a coping strategy and felt isolated during the experience. Those who identified as transgender or were struggling with sexuality felt self-harm compounded the differences they were already feeling.

The way we socialise boys often hinders them from expressing emotional pain in ways perceived as feminine. Expectations of handling life 'like a man' has a huge impact on boys and the way they verbalise pain and seek support.

Jacob, who used to attend Youth Excel's Clinic, was kind enough to talk about his experience. Jacob told me:

> I didn't know of any other boys that self-harmed. Frankly, I thought I was one of a few people in the

world that harmed at the time, and that barely any blokes did because I saw it as mainly a girl thing (thanks Hollywood!). I did it because I just stopped caring, really. I personally don't know any males that self-harm. It's pretty uncommon in my circles.

When I asked a group of boys if males 'self-harm' one answered, 'Depends what you call self-harm. Boys punch things and "end up" breaking their hand. They don't mean to break their hand, but it just happens when you punch something that hard. I don't know if that is self-harm.' When I asked them if they intended to hurt themselves, I got a lot of 'I don't know' responses. Intention defines self-harm, but these boys didn't want to make the association.

I asked Maggie Dent, author, educator and 'champion of boys', to comment on boys' relationship with self-harm. Interestingly, Dent highlighted the natural gravitation boys have to high-risk behaviour, saying, 'Boys hurt themselves a lot – mostly unintentionally and mainly due to impulsive choices looking for fun, risk or the "buzz rush" of excitement, often seeking a victory or a conquest, so that their inner barometer of self-worth gets filled. Boys often see painful moments as a part of growing aka maturation and not so much as a sign of failure.'

She also drew attention to Michael Gurian's work in *Saving our Sons* where he writes about boys' pain thresholds. His description about male biochemistry, brain structure and pain tolerance explains that there are significant gender differences in pain response and in pain tolerance. Dent comments, 'Michael explains that this is part of why males on the average not only feel less pain than females, but actually go out and seek more pain than females.'

A boy's own lack of self-awareness may lead him to jump from feeling to behaviour with little awareness of the thoughts that link the two. It may be very difficult for him to reach out and seek help for a behaviour he perceives as 'normal', or – worse still – the behaviour he is confused or ashamed of. Self-awareness is something that is incredibly important to foster in our young men. Without communication and connection of feelings to thoughts, our boys really are at a disadvantage.

Although I use a lot of stories about girls in this book, I want to keep shedding light on boys who exhibit signs of poor mental health and impulsivity. They may not be fully aware they are using risky behaviour to cope with or express emotional pain or punish themselves. Those boys who are most 'at risk' are those who also lack supportive networks and are limited in their ability to reach out and ask for help. Young men who self-harm are at much higher risk of suicide and therefore of particular concern.

Concluding Thoughts

Self-harm is a highly addictive behaviour that gives both males and females a unique, euphoric sense of control like few other coping strategies. The core understanding that *intent defines self-harm* is important in allowing us to recognise signs of self-harm in young people. Less recognised forms of self-harm can be highly destructive if left undetected and unsupported. In the next chapter I will discuss the psychology and basic physiology of self-harm, and how early intervention can reduce the possibility of it becoming habitual behaviour. To me, this is some of the most important information that parents can receive on the subject of self-harm.

Key Insights from this Chapter

- Most young people deliberately injure themselves in an attempt to cope with, express or control emotional pain. Some use self-harm as a form of self-punishment.
- Self-harm is not 'cutting' but may be any behaviour surrounded by self-destructive thinking. I would also like to point out that it is the intention of the behaviour that classifies self-harm, rather than the behaviour itself.
- Although self-harm may bring temporary relief it is important to note that it does not solve problems.

- Although the link between suicide and self-harm definitely needs to be researched further, there is enough evidence to suggest that self-harm can stand completely independent of suicidal thoughts or actions.
- It is too easy to become familiar with our own children and draw inaccurate conclusions, so an objective opinion is important.
- To many people's surprise, self-harm is not classified as a mental health disorder. It is, however, highly possible that a young person has a mental health disorder at the time that they self-harm.
- I often remind parents that they don't see what they aren't looking for. It is so easy for parents to miss the warning signs of self-harm, especially because self-harm is usually a personal experience, entrenched in secrecy and shame.
- Research certainly suggests strong differences between male and female self-harming tendencies, with males leaning towards high-risk

behaviour and girls tending towards self-injury.

2
The Psychology and Physiology

A school principal called me a few years ago to discuss an alarming trend in her school. 'Self-harm is spreading like cancer,' she said. 'What can you do to help?' She was right. This school, like so many others I was working in, had experienced a sudden rise in students self-harming, with behaviour fuelled by popular students uploading photos of their experiences on the internet.

I investigated the research and tried to make sense of the phenomenon they were facing. Knowing of someone who has self-harmed or made a suicide attempt contributes to risk. In one case study young people who had knowledge of others who self-harmed were 30% more likely to self-harm, indicating peer groups as a key trigger for self-harm.

Time and time again I have seen self-harm come in waves within schools.

I therefore share many schools' concerns about 'copy-cat' occurrences. Too many times I have heard young people tell me that they tried self-harm after a school presentation or workshop. That is why when schools going through a 'self-harm epidemic' ask me to talk to their students about self-harm, I suggest that instead I talk about self-care, resilience and gratitude. Those are the things that foster lasting change.

Eunice first heard about self-harm at school. She writes:

> I first learnt about self-harm in year 8 from school and friends. I remember thinking if other people thought it could help, surely it would help me.

Her mother added:

> There was a talk in year nine at school that she was interested in, but unfortunately it gave her more ideas than help. I was really disappointed with its effect on her.

For Eunice, self-harm very quickly became a habitual part of her life and impacted her greatly.

The vast majority of young people I have mentored have self-harmed because they have seen someone else do it or have had someone suggest it to them. Young people are highly influenced by their peers during adolescence, so they are more likely to try something that is suggested to them by their peers, whether that be 'cutting', taking drugs, drinking alcohol or the like. The company they keep is highly important and does have a huge impact on them. Research confirms that vulnerable people cluster together because of shared stressors.

Boys I have spoken to have told me of the female relationships that have influenced their decision to cut.

Paul, who tried cutting in Year 8, said to me, 'I tried it almost as a way to be popular with girls. The girls talked about cutting every day. It was something that I just did to fit in. It is something I grew out of pretty quickly. I went "emo" for a while there!'

I have also met boys who have looked up to older males who have engaged in high-risk behaviour to deal with emotions that were running high.

By looking up to these males, they learnt to handle their emotions in a similar way. Driving recklessly while in a rage or punching a wall until your hand bleeds may be seen as immaturity, venting or self-harm depending on the lens of the viewer- and ultimately-the intent of the young man.

The Onset of Puberty

I have noticed the onset of puberty is a time that young people often experiment with self-harm. Interestingly enough, a survey featured in the *Self-Harm and Adolescents Report* showed that the onset of self-harm was related to pubertal phase rather than a particular age. It has been suggested that the onset of self-harm is often later in boys than in girls because of the later onset of puberty. The association between self-harm and puberty has been associated with a particular neurodevelopmental vulnerability during this time, with increased risk of emotional instability.

The *Youth Mental Health Report: Youth Survey* also states, 'Adolescence is a period of great change for all young people and can entail a range of physical, social, emotional and academic challenges. It is a time when young people are establishing their identities, seeking greater independence, transitioning to adulthood and often facing pressures from both school and social environments. It is also the peak onset for many mental health disorders.' Young people definitely need additional support during this time as they learn to manage their own wellbeing.

Whether it happens in Year 4, Year 7 or Year 9, the onset of puberty is a big time for young people. Research suggests that girls are particularly vulnerable to cutting during this time. However, puberty usually comes with a range of other influences. Young people, especially girls, may be susceptible to social instability as well. Other factors that significantly increase the risk include depressive symptoms, alcohol misuse, and the onset of sexual activity.

Research from *Self-Harm and Suicide in Adolescents* puts the place of puberty in perspective with other elements that affect a young person's susceptibility to self-harm. It explores the impact of genetic and biological factors, psychiatric disorders, personality factors (like impulsivity, perfectionism and low optimism), exposure to suicide or self-harm in others, the availability of self-harm opportunities to a young person, and negative life events or social problems. Puberty is a time of physical and social change which usually exacerbates all these things.

Amanda's Story

Amanda, now mother of eight children, was gracious enough to share her story with me. Amanda got her periods just before her tenth birthday. Now that is a lot for a young one to deal with! The onset of puberty was a crazy time for her. It sent her whole life, including her mental health, into a spin. She started cutting in Year 6, and in the years to follow she started drinking, smoking and engaging in other risk-taking behaviour.

She recalls being bored 'in her head' around the time she started cutting. One day she sat in her room and decided to pick up a blade and scratch into her arm. She doesn't remember hearing about self-harm from anyone or reading about it in her teen magazines that she loved reading.

Amanda says:

> Looking back, I had very poor mental health from a young age. I needed the hit of endorphins to help me cope, so I used to do other things than just self-harm. I used to steal things too. The only problem was that I needed to "go again" and "go again" so it was a false sense of coping. You aren't coping but you think you are. It's all a cover up. You think it's a coping mechanism, but it isn't at all. It's just because you don't want to deal with what is happening inside.
>
> When I hit puberty, I didn't just start self-harming. I also stopped positive activities like ballet, which I was good at. I thought my legs were fat, and my leotard wasn't

covering enough of my growing body. I didn't want to show my legs, which was funny because the next year I wanted to flaunt them!

It was in Year 4, about ten years old, when everything changed for me.

As I heard her story I recognised other contributing factors beside the early onset of puberty – significant depression in her family history, impulsivity and risk taking really stood out to me. Amanda also endured the death of a loved one when she was nine years old, which she believed had a major impact on her. She loved horror movies and books, and the mental health nurse at the hospital told her parents to throw them out as they thought they were playing a part in her desire to self-harm. That, along with sexual abuse at the age of 11, were factors she felt contributed to her ongoing desire to self-harm. I believe that when these experiences hit in combination with the onset of puberty young people are at a much higher risk.

Amanda has a supportive and loving family that she wants to praise 'all the way to the moon and back'. One thing that Amanda wants to emphasise is that parents can't always be blamed for their children's choices or poor mental health.

Motives for Self-Harm

In saying that, seeing a friend self-harm might trigger self-harming behaviour, but doesn't cause it. An internal motive is the cause of self-harm. Parents need to think of self-harm as non-verbal language to express either a 'cry of pain' or a 'cry for help'. Both cries are valid requests for specific support. Support can be tailor made once parents understand the underlying motive.

Sixty-five percent of young people reported at least one 'cry of help' motive and 87% reported at least one 'cry of pain' motive. These motives were consistent across genders. This indicates to me that the reasons for self-harm can be very wide and therefore not restricted to the list below. Motives for self-harm can also change, depending on the circumstances surrounding self-harm.

Findings from *The Child and Adolescent Self-Harm in Europe (CASE) Study,* helped me a great deal when I ran Youth Excel's Psychology Clinic and was frequently mentoring young people who were self-harming. Being able to hear and recognise their specific 'cries' gave me a huge head start in connecting with young people who came to my office. Once I discovered this, I was well on my way to validating their needs and supporting them.

A 'cry of pain' motive might sound like a young person who wants to:
- get relief from a terrible state of mind
- escape an impossible situation
- punish themselves
- die

A 'cry for help' motive might sound like a young person who wants to:
- show how desperate they are feeling
- frighten someone
- get their own back on someone
- find out if someone really loves them
- get someone's attention

If you have a young person who is self-harming, consider which one (or more) of these motives might be driving their behaviour. If you can determine that, you can tailor your language and support to help meet that need. Remember, a 'cry of pain' or a 'cry for help', rather than cuts on a young person's arm, is what we need to look for.

For example, I have worked with young people who didn't cope well with their parent's decision to remarry. They experienced a strong sense of loss and abandonment. Self-harm was a way of expressing a 'cry for help'. In such cases it was appropriate for parents to acknowledge their young person's feelings and respond specifically, often with the guidance of a third party like a psychologist who could offer nonbiased support. Not an easy process for anyone!

I have also worked with young people who have experienced bullying at school and were expressing a 'cry of pain' through self-harm. Bullying is commonly difficult for young people to talk to adults about and the pain that it causes is often internalised. In such cases, parents may recognise that dealing with the underlying issue may subsequently improve self-harm.

Remember, looking for causes isn't about allocating blame, but understanding motives can help. Poor mental health plus stressful life events (including family issues or personal pain) makes young people more susceptible to self-harm. It is the combination of elements that becomes overwhelming for young people and often leads them to poor coping mechanisms.

Understanding the Psychology

The following common scenario further explains the psychology of self-harm and how a 'cry of pain' or a 'cry for help' interacts with the self-harm process:

> Emma wakes up with heightened emotions. She has lots of assignments due and she hasn't slept well. She goes to school and has a fight with a friend who she

argues with often. She feels alone. Isolated, in fact.

When she arrives home her mind is racing. She tries to watch TV to distract herself, but she can't stop thinking about that friendship and how things always spiral downhill. She blames herself. She turns to social media (good old social media!) where she sees her friend inviting another girl out on the weekend. The feeling of being alone, staying alone and being picked on intensifies. Maybe all her friends feel the same way about her?

She has a shower and listens to music. A warm shower usually calms her down, but this time it doesn't. She starts to cry. She hopes to talk to her mum about her day, but her mum is busy. Her mum has just come in from work with lots on her mind. Her mum says, 'You know what Kirsty is like. Just ignore her and get on with your life. Go and do your homework'.

Over the next 40 minutes things go from bad to worse as Emma cycles between crying, looking at her phone, listening to sad music and back again. She tries to settle herself, but nothing seems to work.

She starts thinking, *I can't cope any more. If this doesn't stop soon I'm going to do something stupid.* For her there is a 'cry of pain' that starts to drive her behaviour. For other young people there may be a 'cry for help' that says, *If I cut, maybe Mum will see how desperate I feel,* or, *If I cut, Kirsty will see how much this is affecting me.*

Young people tell me that they have heard that self-harm works. In Emma's case, Kirsty self-harms and has told Emma that it has been a life saver for her.

Emma takes a blade from her pencil sharpener to cut her thighs. Her body releases endorphins – pain inhibitors. You can liken it to the endorphins that are released after the pain of a good workout or mountain climb. Emma describes an initial high or a rush as these endorphins are released. This signals a change in the chemical state of her body.

Psychologically, a young person's focus turns to the physical pain, the imagery of the blood and the injury. Emma finds that the friendship problems now melt away into the background as secondary issues. The physical pain is a distraction to the emotional pain.

After the rush Emma then reports a low, or a numbing pain that leads to a shut down, exhaustion and crash that throws her body into a recovery period. The knock-on effect of this low is just as addictive as the high. As her body heals, Emma struggles with the guilt and shame associated with her desire to hurt herself. She tries to hide her scars.

Like all destructive behaviour, self-harm is highly addictive because it wires the neurocircuitry or pathways of the brain to reach towards self-harm for relief. The more times young people cut, the stronger the 'stress + cutting = relief' circuit becomes.

In *The Functions of Self-injury in Young Adults,* Klonsky explains how participants tended to feel overwhelmed, sad and frustrated before self-injury, and calm after self-injury. These affective changes predict lifetime frequency of self-injury, suggesting that they reinforce behaviour.

In the next section, I share some insights about how the adolescent brain interacts with self-harm differently once it adopts it as a routine coping strategy. This, to me, is some of the most important information that parents can understand.

The Physiology of Self-Harm

I have spent time in hospitals working with young people who have mutilated their bodies for years. I have also spent time sitting with Year 8 girls who have 'scratched their wrists' for the first time. I have seen boys as young as six continually and deliberately injure themselves during tantrums. I have also seen young people try self-harm once, come to a counselling centre for support, and never return to it. I have supported both short term, mild self-harmers and lifelong, chronic self-harmers.

One of the questions I have always asked myself is this: When and how does self-harm become an uncontrollable habit?

Before I go any further, I want to stop and define two terms I will use: 'voluntary self-harm' and 'habitual self-harm'.

I use the term 'voluntary self-harm' as a way of describing behaviour that is a young person's conscious and deliberate action. This type of behaviour is very goal orientated.

I use the term 'habitual self-harm' as a way of describing self-harm that is a young person's automatic, routine or habitual response. This type of behaviour has become an addiction.

Any voluntary behaviour that is followed by a reward is reinforced. With repeated engagement and consistent reward, the behaviour goes from being voluntary to habitual. Self-harm can become a young person's 'go-to response' to manage stress or emotional pain.

Interestingly, voluntary and habitual self-harm are processed differently by the brain. Voluntary self-harm behaviour is processed in the part of the brain known as ventral striatum, which primarily enables rewards, cognition, reinforcement and motivation when young people engage in voluntary self-harm behaviours.

A voluntary self-harmer's body will function in a very similar way as it normally does. Self-harm is still fear provoking and physically painful. Their pain management system is not yet compromised. Young people are not fully associating as a 'self-harmer'.

When this behaviour becomes habitual, more activation in the dorsal striatum can be observed. Habitual self-harm behaviour is now activating the part of the brain that mediates cognition involving motor function, inhibitory control and stimulus response learning.

Once self-harm has become a habitual behaviour it becomes tightly associated with a certain situation or feeling, and it becomes the young person's first response when this situation or feeling arises. It can even be automatically and routinely triggered by specific cues or circumstances. For example, it may be young people's first response when they feel stressed, out of control or sad. They may also identify themselves as a 'self-harmer' and become desensitised to the fear and pain.

There are proposed physiological reasons why habitual self-harm is less fear provoking and physically painful than voluntary self-harm. A compelling reason for this higher pain threshold is abnormal levels of endogenous opioids, a group of hormones that is linked to our brain's pain-relief mechanisms. The relationship between endogenous opioids and pain perception has been extensively researched.

Recent studies have also shown that individuals who self-harm have different biochemistry – specifically, endogenous opioids levels – compared to those who do not self-harm. This results in the body's pain management system being compromised. A young person's pain threshold for self-harm increases, meaning that self-harm becomes almost effortless. They would also have to harm themselves more intensely in order achieve the same outcome.

In my work with young people, I have consistently seen that self-harmers have a higher pain threshold the more they self-harm. I have also noticed that less effort is required to engage in self-harm over time, as the individual increasingly identifies with the behaviour and their tolerance for it increases. Eunice, one of my previous clients, explains in her words, 'After a year of self-harm, I began building a tolerance to the pain. I needed to feel more harm to numb me from what was going on with my depression and anxiety'.

As parents and caring adults, it is important that we understand that there is a difference between voluntary and habitual self-harm behaviour, as it will determine how we respond and support them. I am particularly passionate about catching self-harm in its early stages, as this is when it is most responsive to intervention. The changeover happens at a different time for every young person and depends on a range of factors, including the frequency and intensity of their self-harm, and their personal vulnerability.

The genetic disposition for habitual self-harm has been tentatively suggested by some researchers. However, there is currently not enough research evidence to determine conclusively whether this is the case. Prevention of self-harm will be greatly aided with future research into this idea.

Concluding Thoughts

The earlier we can connect and communicate with young people about self-harm and associated poor mental health, the better chance we have of intervening at a time when self-harm is still voluntary. I have dedicated the upcoming chapters to communication and connection, as this is where real change starts. I want to answer, in a very practical way, what parents are to do when they first find out their son or daughter is self-harming, and how they should continue to support a young person through their journey to good health. But first, let's talk about the role of the internet.

Key Insights from this Chapter

- Knowing of someone who has self-harmed or made a suicide attempt contributes to risk. In one case study young people who had knowledge of others who self-harmed were 30% more likely to self-harm, indicating peer groups as a key trigger for self-harm.
- The association between self-harm and puberty has been associated with a particular neurodevelopmental vulnerability during this time, with increased risk of emotional instability.
- Young people can be expressing both a 'cry of pain' and a 'cry for help' when self-harming.
- Looking for causes isn't about allocating blame, but understanding motives can help.
- Poor mental health plus stressful life events (including family issues or personal pain) makes young people more susceptible • to self-harm. It is the combination of

elements that becomes overwhelming for young people and often leads them to poor coping mechanisms.
- Like all destructive behaviour, self-harm is highly addictive because it wires the neurocircuitry or pathways of the brain to reach towards self-harm for relief.
- The more times young people cut, the stronger the 'stress + cutting = relief' circuit becomes.
- Any voluntary behaviour that is followed by a reward is reinforced. With repeated engagement and consistent reward, the behaviour goes from being voluntary to habitual.

3
The Role of the Internet

A deputy principal of a primary school spoke to me about her frustration when talking to parents about self-harm. 'It is my job to bring self-harm to parents' attention,' she said. 'Parents quickly brush it off as just "attention seeking" when it could be the precursor to something much bigger. They seem blindsided by the seriousness of it. I had to speak to two parents this year. Both parents said it was nothing and "she doesn't mean anything by it." That concerned me.'

Primary teachers regularly tell me stories of little ones – as young as nine and ten years old – who are breaking their sharpeners, taking the blades out and cutting their legs under their school desks. I am both intrigued and shocked by the age of these children.

After asking how the school deals with such a sensitive issue with children so young, one teacher explained, 'We spoke to them one on one, asked them direct questions and went from there. They didn't mind talking about it. The little ones are easier to confront than teenagers. They know that adults are going to ask them tricky questions and they don't have ready-made answers. They haven't learnt how to hide things yet. They have a higher level of trust in adults. We can say to them that self-harm is not the answer, and we can set up some support for them because they trust us. When they are little, teachers have such a lot of influence.'

When these teachers are asked why they think children so young are self-harming, the internet is the first to be blamed, 'Young kids are open to so much with Netflix and YouTube and shows like *13 Reasons Why*. There is no filter and no-one sitting over their shoulder. That's the issue. They learn a whole lot more, so much earlier. Those producers are trying to meet the needs of the market!'

It is really important that parents keep an eye out for early exposure to self-harm, as little people can experiment with 'grown up' ways to express and manage their emotions. If parents keep their eyes and ears open they will notice self-harm featured in current affairs, movies and television shows. There will be limits to the graphic nature of the content depending on the censorship guidelines and media regulations associated with each country and broadcaster. However, it doesn't take much to trigger an idea in a young person who may be particularly vulnerable at that given time.

One mother told me:

> We use to watch *Home and Away* (a popular Australian soap opera) religiously. I grew up watching it, and so had continued the same with my daughters. Everything stopped or was done by 7p.m. so we could watch the show. This one episode had a young girl sleeping on the lounge in front of the TV and her brother came home. He sees that her skirt is sitting a little high and goes to pull it down to a modest place and put a blanket over her legs. This is when

he notices the self-harming cuts on her upper thigh. Cutting seemed to be a hot topic on teen TV shows and discussed amongst kids at school. We have a gut feeling that this is where our daughter got the idea of cutting to deal with her frustrations.

Netflix is of particular concern because of the different censorship guidelines associated with each program. The blogging and social networking website Tumblr is known to be the active platform for self-harm content. Half of all posts on Tumblr related to self-harm are images. The lack of moderation by this site, together with anonymity and an open forum, makes it easy to share the most severe and dark side of self-harm unfiltered.

Messaging app Snapchat is a perfect platform for self-harm images to be shared. The limited life span of photos sent ('snaps') makes them easier for young people to hide from parents. Photo-sharing app Instagram is also frequently used by self-harmers. If any 'inappropriate' hashtags become blocked with a 'can we help?' message, they are quickly replaced with another alternative from the self-harm community.

Keywords and hashtags are the most popular ways that young people search for content, share images and congregate around self-harm. For a better understanding of how those congregating around self-harm are using Instagram in potentially destructive ways, you may want to google these hashtags: #selfharmmm #blithe #cat #blood #selfinjuryy #mysecretfamily #secretsociety123 #depression #thinspo (anorexia) #proanna (anorexia) #deb (depression) #annie (anxiety) #olive (obsessive compulsive disorder). Note that they are intentionally misspelt to avoid being blocked.

The internet is in a constant state of flux. Self-harm websites and forums are regularly updated, created and deleted. Once highly popular sites, when shut down, are quickly replaced by others. No sooner do adults block one site, than young people move on to another site. This fluidity makes it a challenge to protect young people from destructive content. There is no doubt that parents feel at a loss as to how to manage and protect young people struggling with self-harm when they go online.

Benefits and Dangers

More than half (51.3%) of young people who report self-harm have previously engaged in internet searches for self-harm or suicide-related material. The *Youth Mental Health Report: Youth Survey* also indicates that the top three places young people with probable serious mental illness go to for help are friends, parents and the internet – as opposed to friends, parents and relatives/family friends for those without. Although some research cited the role of the internet in young people's self-harm in the commencement of their behaviour, most reported that young people engaged with the internet to make sense of their thoughts and self-harm behaviour. The internet was an addition to self-harm, rather than a catalyst for it. As discussed in earlier chapters, base line vulnerability is the precursor to self-harm.

There is no doubt that the internet can provide benefits including help seeking, stress alleviation, coping strategies and forums reinforcing positive relationships. As Jacob, a young man who used cutting as a coping mechanism through high school told me:

> I've had a positive experience with the internet as a whole. I've met lifelong friends through it, talked about mental health issues and helped others through them, and helped give them a better understanding about it. I have no doubt that the internet has had a negative effect on some, but I personally haven't had that experience.

However, internet interactions have an overwhelmingly negative impact on participants: normalising self-harm, revealing self-harm techniques and encouraging concealment. It often amplifies the severity of the methods, techniques and frequency of self-harm.

Many local schools share the same views and concerns, confirming research. One local guidance officer said, 'Young people can be relatively naïve when they first try self-harm. Some young people see it for the first time on the internet and experiment with scratches on their arm, leg or stomach, relatively innocently. What concerns me is that some experimental newcomers start to associate with "hardcore" self-harmers and expose themselves to issues they wouldn't otherwise associate with.'

Kate's Story

Kate struggled with both self-harm and eating disorders, and found that she had to significantly change her online presence and activities in order to break destructive patterns. The internet exposed her to a variety of negative influences and relationships at critical times in her life journey. Here is her story:

> When I was 14 I would go through massive lows. I lived at boarding school so people thought that I was just missing home. I was just a quiet kid in most people's books. I wasn't very good at processing emotion by nature, and that made me more vulnerable to

poor methods of coping. As a way of processing emotions, I would self-harm and engage in eating disorder behaviours. I used both of these methods to cope at boarding school. No one noticed until I was in Year 11. I was able to hide it for two years.

When I was 18 I lived rurally, and I didn't have a lot of contact with people my own age. This is where the internet really had an impact on me. The most contact I had was with people I worked with. One of them was close to my age, but the rest of them were more than ten years older than I was. For me it become kind of a way of reaching out for support and help. I had no one I could share what was going on in my head and the online community was a place I could turn to.

It very quickly became toxic. I started using the internet to find ways to lose weight faster, how to exercise, and different ways to self-harm and hide self-harm from people. It became a way of educating myself. I made "friends" but "friends" is the wrong word. I was introduced to people who encouraged me to choose really bad coping strategies. Encouragement only spurred us on further.

I am now 23 years old. I have been diagnosed with bipolar and I am well managed. I have to self-care every day. I am still not great at it, but I am learning. I have a good care team around me and a good support system. I trust them and at times I have to rely on them. Medication is a part of my management. I have good friends who I play sport with. They constantly encourage me to get better.

I have a much healthier online presence. I think that has got to do with my maturing. I also deleted my old Instagram account. I had to start with a clean slate. It was about recovery for me and not about the illnesses that I had. I have to be careful who I follow and who follows me. I manage my profile well. Living with self-harm and an eating disorder is not the most fun life and I had to do something.

The Power of Strong Images

Another reason that the internet is so powerful is that strong images have the capacity to induce a physical reaction that invokes a desire to engage in them. Research clearly tells us that there is a very visual aspect to self-harm, and the sight of blood or a bruise is an important part of the process.

Research suggests that online imagery in itself has the ability to:
- bring back memories of previous self-harming episodes
- cause a young person to envisage how others would experience the act
- inspire a young person to re-create practices presented by images
- cause a young person to compete with the severity or techniques of the self-harm seen on an image

- scold a young person for not engaging in forms of self-harm presented in images
- create a reliance on images to trigger a self-harm session

When young people go looking for this imagery or have friends who show it to them, it has a very strong emotional connection for them. I have met young people who have had not been able to 'shake' images of self-harm until they have performed the same act in the real world.

Digital Footprint

I am also concerned about the digital footprint young people who have experienced self-harm or mental health challenges are leaving. I have worked with many 14-year-olds who have posted unsightly images of self-harm in the name of self-expression. Years later, often when these young people are in their early twenties and in a healthier head space, they have contacted me again and expressed their concern about images resurfacing. They now understand the stigma that mental health has in the community and realise that their jobs and relationships could be greatly impacted if images resurface.

Susan McLean, one of Australia's leading cyber safety experts, was good enough to talk with me on the topic. She said, 'Once you put it there, it's there forever. You can't get it back. The reality is you can't ring Facebook and say, "Can you pull it down?" But when young people aren't in a good head space, none of that matters to them.'

Unfortunately, I have seen young people send self-harm images to friends in confidence through apps like Snapchat, which pride themselves on the transient nature of photos, only to discover that the 'snap' has been screenshot and put out there for the world to see. The harsh reality that the web is a public place only hits home for most young people when things go wrong.

McLean also said, 'The "right to be forgotten" law has been introduced in Europe. We don't always follow European law but there may be a groundswell for new data protection laws change in Australia. For now, all we have is prevention. This puts a lot of onus back on clinicians who are working with young people. We have to remind them of their digital footprint at times when it is not on the forefront of their minds.'

What fades quicker – a scar on a young person's arm or a post of self-harm? I guess that depends which country you live in!

Strategic Responses to Self-Harm

The internet is entwined in almost every issue that families face, self-harm being no exception. We can't deny its power and influence in our homes. That is why I strongly urge parents of pre-teens to set up young people's online life in a manner that can withstand the rockiest of the teenage years. It is critical that we educate ourselves as parents and have a strong plan for our kids' digital journey from the beginning.

That being said, I know I am speaking to an audience whose children may have full autonomy online. It is much more difficult perhaps impossible – to manage the content once they have this independence. It can be very distressing for parents who are no longer able to enforce rules or boundaries, especially when they know their child is in an unhealthy state of mind. However, parents – allow me to say this—please realise that if you are paying the bill, you still have more control than you may realise!

When parents first find out their child is self-harming, they have to work through a range of initial emotions. During that process, parents usually re-evaluate their parenting strategies and styles. Sometimes this means they make big changes to the way they are managing and monitoring their young person and technology in the home. That is appropriate and normal.

There are some basic approaches I have seen parents take in response to self-harm. I have noticed that each of these approaches is woven throughout the stories in this book, depending on the parenting styles of the families. There is nothing conclusively right or wrong about any of these approaches!

In fact, the right help at the wrong time is the *wrong* help, so professional advice and personal judgement are critical. Balance is usually a good thing in life, even when it comes to parenting. Stay flexible.

The first approach is the 'increased control' approach. Parents may control the home environment by enforcing stricter online controls. They may also take away objects that could be used to harm. Some parents fear this approach may provoke backlash. Other parents find it difficult to maintain in the long term. Its effectiveness may be limited because behavioural change isn't initiated by the young person but is driven by the parent.

There are times when increased control and management of the internet is necessary, as triggers for self-harm are real. It is important that we keep our homes safe, positive spaces, especially during times of vulnerability. I would, however, advise that parents tackle one change at a time, to reduce resistance to change. Even one change will feel like a big deal to a young person. Simple things like designating tech-free zones (the dinner table, bathrooms and bedrooms after 9p.m.) can make a big impact. Again, this will depend on the severity of the situation, and should not replace your own judgement.

The second approach is a 'keep a close eye' approach. This is where you attempt to keep existing boundaries consistent but increase your watchful eye and communication. The aim is to treat a young person as per normal, making sure expectations for going to school and doing chores at home stay the same as much as possible. Exceptions to the normal routine are made when necessary. Relationship time is usually increased. Some families go so far as to insist on checking or monitoring devices but still allow them to be used without additional restrictions.

It's important to acknowledge that there is a lot you can't control when it comes to young people's online life. If you find yourself stuck when it comes to controlling technology, ask yourself, *What can I do?* rather than *What can't I do?* The important thing is to find positive alternatives and then surround your children with those positives.

I suggest parents put ten real-world activities on the fridge and encourage young people to choose them instead of screen time as often as possible. The list of self-care strategies are good options for young people to choose from.

High school teacher and mother of two, Renee Bennett, says, 'I have to take responsibility for giving my children alternative options to being alone on their screen. It is definitely work on my part. I have to give them as many experiences outside of the house as I can. As a family we have never taken screens with us when we leave the house.'

She also says, 'Getting them around older people with similar (positive) values has also helped. That is where youth groups and older role models are great. Sports coaches, uncles, aunties and neighbours are powerful in kids' lives. Good advice is always cooler from them than coming from Mum or Dad.'

The third approach is the 'meet their needs'. This is a really common response to self-harm, where parents go to great lengths to accommodate their child. An example might be allowing them to stay up all night on their phone because they can't sleep. There is often the expectation that in meeting a child's needs they will not feel the need to self-harm. However, that is seldom the reality. Some parents have found this approach makes young people more self-indulgent and not accountable to their potential. This approach therefore does have its limitations, especially if it is not delivered in a balanced way.

Initially, parents may feel like they have to walk on eggshells and avoid conflict at all costs. Some parents even report that their young person used a threat of self-harm to get their own way or maintain control. This changes the balance of power in the home and makes parents feel manipulated. It is important that parents learn to be more assertive with their child again and not be afraid to parent.

My advice is this: be the parent! Don't let fear or your young person's moods control your judgement.

There is always a fine line between mental health and normal teenage behaviour. That line is one that can leave parents questioning themselves. What is important to remember is, even the most well-balanced teenagers try to manipulate their parents and at times their parents have to say 'no'.

Shared Images

As a society we are communicating more than we ever have before, but the type of communication we engage in is different from how it has been in previous generations. In today's world, face-to-face communication makes up a small part of young people's communication. That means that young people need different skills to navigate their relationships. My concern is that we aren't educating them to deal with the challenges they are facing online.

'We are also seeing situations where young people are using threats of suicide to emotionally blackmail their friends on a daily basis. Texts like, "If you unfriend me I will kill myself" are very common,' says McLean. 'I am also hearing young people say, "If you show anyone else that image (referring to self-harm or binge drinking) I will kill myself" – trapping the young person into secrecy.' McLean's greatest immediate concern is for mentally well kids who do not have the tools to deal with these situations.

Last week McLean heard from a girl whose mental health was under stress and strain because her friend was talking to her about self-harming. She was worried she wouldn't be considered a good friend if she shared it with an adult. She was afraid to tell her mum and dad how she was feeling. 'You can't allow it to be all encompassing. You have to be prepared to speak up and tell someone about it,' McLean told the young lady.

I feel young people are ill-equipped to navigate the psychological complexity of online relationships. Young people are not always mature enough to call manipulation what it is, and fear not responding or not going along with their friends. For this reason, parents need to be aware of young people's moods, subtle changes in relationship habits and online communication, understanding that some of the issues they may be dealing with online are potentially life threatening.

Julie is 15 years old and attends a school in Brisbane. She shares with me one of her school friend's Instagram accounts. He is a friend she takes pride in supporting.

Someone who I have known for four years has a lot of photos on his Instagram of his cuts on his arms, drugs, smoking, pills and depression quotes. There are some cuts that he needed stitches for. It hurts him, but he can't cry. It is a private account, but everyone shows people because it is so explicit. I'm just here to be his friend.

People don't know what he has gone through, but I know he has gone through a lot. It was all because of one girl. She used to tell him to go and kill himself all the time. She used to break up with him and then get back with him on the same day. She messed with his head so much and now he is messed up. His parents take him to a psychologist every Wednesday. I know that he has mental health issues. His mother thinks that there is nothing she can do about his Instagram. They try and monitor it but it's not working. He can hide everything online.

I'm not here to tell him what to do, I'm just here to listen sometimes. People say I am good at that. He needs someone his own age to talk to sometimes. I know he has adults that are there too and I would tell someone if I needed to.

But not everyone handles it as well as Julie appears to.

Louise Klar, a student counsellor who has worked with those who have self-harmed for over a decade, says, 'Snapchat has enabled young people to share self-harm without fear of adults seeing it. This enables young people to handle issues between themselves without adult intervention. However, what young people forget is that the image is "real-time blood" coming up on their friend's screen. So often young people don't realise the person on the other end could be really distressed.'

McLean also shares the impact that graphic images are having on young people who don't self-harm, with alarming stories of shared images being common place. 'Young people may be reaching out for help, but their friends aren't the right people to help them,' McLean states. 'Young people can find images very distressing and scary. They flounder and wonder who they should be telling ... and *am I even a good friend if I tell someone?*'

Young people who are accustomed to self-harm may not realise the effect that it could have on the viewer. Often the person seeing the image of self-harm hasn't tried self-harm themselves. Some young people do an amazing job of comforting each other whilst others find it quite daunting. Here is a list of suggestions that I give young people to help them support friends who are going through a tough time. It is not easy for them to set boundaries, love unconditionally and also look after their own needs. These are mature skills that adults struggle with at times.

Things Friends Should Do:
- Listen and care about their feelings but then move on and talk about normal things
- Do normal activities together
- If you are worried about their safety talk to an adult
- Never promise not to tell an adult
- Realise everyone has their limits. If you feel stressed, talk to an adult
- Encourage your friend to get professional support if they don't have it already. You may want to go with them to a school counsellor to help them take that step
- Make a pact with your friend that allows you to contact an adult (who you both agree on) if you are ever concerned about their safety
- If you receive a message or an image that disturbs you, screen shot it and contact an adult

Things Friends Shouldn't Do:
- Try and be their parent or counsellor
- Push confessions or conversations about self-harm

- Make them talk to an adult
- Increase the drama by talking to other friends
- Show other friends the texts or images
- Ignore them or the self-harm

Concluding Thoughts

The online world provides further opportunities for young people to educate and express themselves as well as support each other, often independently of adults. We have the great challenge of staying connected to young people's online life and educating ourselves so we stay relevant in their lives. The next chapter is dedicated to the new phenomenon of digital self-harm, an online version of self-harm.

Key Insights from this Chapter

- More than half (51.3%) of young people who report self-harm have previously engaged in internet

searches for self-harm or suicide-related material.
- It is really important that parents keep an eye out for early exposure to self-harm content. It doesn't take much to trigger an idea in a young person who may be particularly vulnerable at that given time.
- The internet can provide benefits including help seeking, stress alleviation, coping strategies and forums reinforcing positive relationships. However, internet interactions have an overwhelmingly negative impact on participants: normalising self-harm, revealing self-harm techniques and encouraging concealment. It often amplifies the severity of the methods, techniques and frequency of self-harm.
- Another reason that the internet is so powerful is that strong images have the capacity to induce a physical reaction that invokes a desire to engage in them.
- I am concerned about the digital footprint young people who have experienced self-harm or mental

health challenges are leaving. What fades quicker – a scar on a young person's arm or a post of self-harm?
- It's important to acknowledge that there is a lot you can't control when it comes to young people's online life. If you find yourself stuck when it comes to controlling technology, ask yourself, *What can I do?* rather than *What can't I do?*
- There is always a fine line between mental health and normal teenage behaviour.
- What is important to remember is, even the most well-balanced teenagers try to manipulate their parents and at times their parents have to say 'no'. My advice when it comes to managing technology is – be the parent even if it is unpopular.

4

Digital Self-Harm

Digital self-harm is a relatively new phenomenon about which there is little public awareness. Although research is still emerging and there are many questions yet to be answered, this chapter provides my current findings from interviews with experts, young people, parents and schools. The intensely private nature of this topic means that further information will continue to surface over time.

This year I have had a few opportunities to personally support young people who have digitally self-harmed, as well as schools and parents who have suspected digital self-harm. Each time, I have realised the gravity of the issue and complexities facing this generation. I have gained greater empathy and a deeper understanding of the overall psychological needs of this generation.

In my research I found that digital self-harm was an area that young people were far more aware of than adults. When a local mum asked her 12- and 14-year-olds whether they had heard of 'kids bullying themselves online' they responded, 'Yeah they do it to get attention.' She was shocked by their cold and matter-offact reaction, especially as she had never heard the term 'digital self-harm' before. My interactions with many school staff and professionals reflect the same tone.

Unfortunately, I personally believe the online variation of self-harm is yet to fully surface in homes and schools. With 35% of young people saying that digital self-harm achieved what they wanted it to achieve, I anticipate it will be a strategy that continues to rise in popularity.

Because of this it is critical that parents and professionals are aware and forearmed to tackle conversations, as the consequences may be catastrophic if we are not prepared.

What is Digital Self-Harm?

Digital self-harm is known as the online variant of self-harm. It is also called self-cyberbullying, cyber self-harm or self-trolling. Digital self-harm is the posting or sharing of demeaning information about oneself anonymously online.

Digital self-harm can be a single comment or hundreds of comments on a young person's Instagram feed, through SMS, email, social media, gaming consoles, web forums or any other online platform that can be conceived. Comments can be posted by fake screen names, 'handles' and aliases made up by a young person. Examples of comments might be, 'If u only knew how much ur boyfriend hated u', 'u r fat', 'don't come and sit with us tomorrow', 'no one likes you anyway', 'u are a useless waste of space', 'your new haircut looks disgusting', and 'u think you are something special but u aren't.'

Think of a young person in their room at night alone, using a few fake accounts to bully themselves with hateful comments. Their friends see those comments and have a chance to respond to them, both defending them or even encouraging the bullying. The young person may continue these fake exchanges with themselves until late into the night! Sometimes a young person then will approach the school guidance officer or trusted friends in an attempt to reach out for help for the online bullying – which they are the author of.

Hannah Smith's Story

This behaviour first entered the public spotlight in 2013 when it was revealed that 14-year-oldHannah Smith, from Leicestershire, England, had anonymously sent damaging messages to herself on the social media platform Ask.fm. This was done in the weeks leading up to her suicide. At the time, her family believed she was driven to suicide by bullies. Her father even spoke out against trolls, which sparked conversations about cyberbullying on social media sites around the world. However, the world was shocked when a police investigation found that she had posted 98% of the comments herself.

There is no doubt that Hannah had been bullied before. Her family recalls a time when her head was repeatedly hit against a wall at a party. Research suggests that a precursor for bullying others is having been bullied. A lot of work has already been done in schools to combat bullying and we must continue to stand strong in this area so that the cycle of abuse is broken. I believe that programs that empower young people to deal with bullying as it happens are critical.

What We Know

Hannah's tragic death caught the attention of researchers Dr Justin Patchin and Dr Sameer Hinduja. They had spent the last decade researching cyberbullying but had never heard of teens cyberbullying themselves. They decided to ask 5500 young American people if they had ever anonymously posted something online about themselves that was mean.

Their staggering results were published in the *Journal of Adolescent Health*. They found that approximately

6% of adolescents aged 12 to 17 engage in digital self-harm. Other surveys have found that approximately 9% of young people engage in the practice. While these percentages seem not very large, they do indicate a problem when extrapolated out to the millions of teens in the America. Although there is limited research in this area, digital self-harm is something we need to be aware of as parents, as its participation rates mirror those of traditional self-harm.

I was very fortunate to be able to interview Dr Hinduja, co-founder of the Cyberbullying Research Centre, about his research and thoughts on this topic. The link between self-harm and digital self-harm cannot be denied. Dr Hinduja explains, 'We specifically found that those who had previously engaged in traditional self-harming behaviours were significantly more likely to engage in digital self-harm. This begs the question as to whether digital self-harm can lead to the same consequences since it is rooted in the same motivations and emotional dysphoria. More research, of course, is necessary.'

The duration of digital self-harm compared to traditional self-harm is interesting to consider. According to Elizabeth Englander's research, 26% of young people do it once, 26% of young people have one ongoing episode, 23% continue for more than a month and only 28% digitally self-harm for between one and two years. That means for approximately 75% of young people, experimentation with digital self-harm is relatively short lived. In saying that, I need to point out that the impact on reputation may be significant and ongoing for young people. A digital 'scar' certainly has the capacity to last as long as a physical scar.

Research consistently show males engaging in higher rates of digital self-harm than females. This is fascinating to me, given that in my small scope of work within Australia I am seeing females engage in digital self-harm at much higher rates than males, and the youth I interviewed for this chapter have consistently viewed it as a female issue. The anonymous nature and broader scope of these surveys may be one reason why males rate higher.

One example I came across was a young man of 13 years old who posted a photo of his newly shaved head as his profile picture. He then used an alias account to comment, saying, 'retard'. This triggered a flood of comments. Lots of people insulted him, and a few girls came to his rescue. Most of his mates stayed out of it and avoided the conversation altogether, thinking the whole thing was 'fishy'. He later told his close mates that he did it for a joke. I wonder if he had concerns about his new haircut and wanted to see what others thought of it before he went to school. We need to be aware of the possibility of males communicating their needs through humour.

Underlying Chat Culture

When I was talking to school staff about digital self-harm, I encountered a lot of discussion about dark humour and online banter (especially on gaming platforms) that normalised degrading speech. Teachers and school staff believed that 'the way young people speak to each other' was affecting those whose mental health was already struggling, and 'laid a foundation' for more psychological games to be played.

Carl Hotko, high school e-safety coordinator and father of three, has a strong interest in this area. He says, 'What is so horrible about the digital world, is dark humour is what they learn. Self-deprecating humour starts with the way they talk to each other and it has to cross over with the way they talk to themselves.'

The anonymous nature of chats and the illusion of distance all amplified their concerns. One staff member who was also a father said to me, 'We have an open doors policy and a very small home. I consider us a very protective family. Even with my own son, when he is playing games with his friends, he turns into a different person with a different voice. The screen is creating a distance and I notice he is far harsher with his words.'

He continues, 'The violence on the screen changes him. When he comes off we are concerned that the violence doesn't turn off. The threads and comments section fill kids' minds with a validation that this type of language is normal. It could easily cross the line to, "If people speak to me like this then it must be okay to speak to myself like this". It normalises it.'

Popular pages like Reddit's 'RoastMe' enable people to post a picture or video, while participants anonymously give the best insults they can – in the name of 'fun'. This is a perfect example of an online culture that encourages young people to look for and hand out cruel insults. Young people have developed a 'code of speech' that is only acceptable online, and not in their everyday speech. However, how realistic is it for young people to make clear boundaries between fantasy and reality?

One mum of a primary school boy messaged me and said, 'Kids have their mind go to this type of language, whether in fun as slang or for real? I worry about what impact the self-talk has in the long run, and how we can get our kids to not speak in such flippant ways about something so serious. If we say in slang "go kill yourself" long enough, will this make a difference in their decisions as they reach puberty?'

Yes, I think it will. We talk a lot about protecting children from a highly sexualised world – and rightly so, as pornography is so accessible to young people these days. We also talk about protecting children from paedophiles and making sure we are aware of who they are 'friending' and following online. But I would like to add and emphasise that we also need to protect them from negativity. Our kids are entitled to an optimistic childhood that gives them the best possibility of entering puberty in a positive state of mind. They need that to get them through the teenage years!

Motives for Digital Self-Harm

Times have changed, with online options for processing pain becoming a reality, but the base line drivers of human nature haven't. What motivates self-harm and digital self-harm are closely linked.

Dr Patchin and Dr Hinduja's research suggests different motives for male and female digital self-harm. Interestingly, girls self-harmed to prove they could handle it, encourage others to worry, or get attention from adults. Girls also most often reported cyberbullying because they were depressed or in emotional pain. Boys did it because they were mad at someone and wanted to start a fight. Boys, however, also admitted they did it sometimes as a joke, although there were usually more serious reasons behind it. Below I will explore some of the key motives I have discussed in interviews with young people and youth workers or other professionals.

A Need to Validate Self-Loathing: Seeking validation from others is something that we all do, especially during low periods. A father with a keen interest in the technical space also commented, 'I guess people have always been able to ask for validation during low periods, but they have never been able to do it on this scale and in such a sneaky way. The mind games that kids are playing with themselves in order to belong has to take them to a darker place. It can't be good for them.'

A Need to Appear Strong: With so many celebrities standing strong in the face of trolling, and receiving praise for standing up to their bullies, young people may want to be seen in the same light. Digital self-harm gives them the opportunity to do so. Sixteen-year-old Sara said to me, 'We look up to people who fight bullies, so it is pretty natural for people to want to boast about getting bullied. Digital self-harm gives teenagers a way to be instant celebrities.'

A Need for Attention: Many young people flat out perceive digital self-harm as a desire for attention. Matt says, 'I think it is because of peoples' families. They don't get any attention at home anymore because everyone is doing their own stuff. Some kids don't care how they are getting attention as long as they are. Drama is how people entertain themselves these days. It's a new addiction.'

To Have Fun: Some young people report digitally self-harming for fun or to relieve boredom. 'I was bored and did it for a joke. I just wanted to see what would happen,' explained Josh. As discussed previously, online banter may be a trigger for digital self-harm. One youth worker explained, 'It's hard to know where the line is with boys especially. We want to believe boys when they are joking by putting themselves down, but it's just their self-talk popping out.'

Exposing Bullies: Young people may use digital self-harm to highlight their real-life needs, especially if they are being bullied. 'I remember bullying at school. Often kids who had low self-esteem or stood out as being different would be bullied the most. There was little they could do about it. Given the safety of potential anonymity on the internet, I can see how kids may feel like they suddenly have power against a bully. They can write and say anything without owning the comment. They can also bully themselves to highlight they are being bullied,' says Charmaine.

A Need to See Who is in My Corner: Digital self-harm may be a way for young people to trigger compliments or insults in order to see who their real friends are. Demi says, 'A lot of young people create fake accounts on Instagram, and they send themselves messages degrading their friendship, saying stuff like, "Demi doesn't like you. She talks about you behind your back." It is a lot of psychological stuff with young people these days. They mess with each other's minds.'

The Social Response to Digital Self-Harm

The social response to online bullying is interesting. According to a special report in *Business Insider,* 30% will join with the bully but 60% will attack the bully. Dr Hinduja believes that bystanders are more comfortable speaking up online than in person where there may be immediate fear of retribution. He also says, 'It's becoming socially "cool" to speak up online.'

The social reaction to digital self-harm is the big difference between it and traditional self-harm. It's on a public platform, whereas traditional self-harm is hidden. The 30% who attack the 'bully' may cause significant issues (online and at school), doing damage to reputations and relationships. The aggressive tactics of the minority have stunned me!

In any schoolyard, the competition for attention is real. There is a limited amount of energy and everyone is fighting for it. If you go online, say between 4 and 7p.m. any school night, the competition for attention is even more real. The louder you are online, the more attention you get. The more likes and comments you get, the more power and affirmation you receive. Power on social media transfers socially. Talk online transfers back to the playground and that is why the online world is the economy of this generation.

I have personally seen motives such as siphoning friends' loyalties, eliciting pity and gaining attention after a big social fallout as key reasons for digital self-harm. Unfortunately, all of these motives usually backfire because young people themselves are wising up to the possibility digital self-harm.

Amy's Story

This is a story I was told by Amy, who is 16 years old. A girl in her class who we will call Jen was 'caught' by her friend for digital self-harming. She was 'called out' in front of the whole grade. This is the story through Amy's eyes:

> Jen got 'sent' this message and then she showed everyone. It was hate from someone anonymous. Her friends offered to help her find their IP address, so she could track them. In my school I haven't heard anything about boys doing it. It is always quite shocking when I hear about how kids do it, and it is surprising who does it.
>
> The last time I heard of it, it was a girl who sits in a quieter group, and she sent herself a message telling herself to kill herself. She played it up extensively. She went around telling everyone. If there was a situation when she didn't want to do her school work she would burst into tears and then blame the text

saying, 'I have a lot going on right now. I can't do my work. I have to leave class and go to the office.'

If she was having a sleepover party and people couldn't make it, she would say, 'You all want me to kill myself too. You all think the same of me.' She was playing that card a lot.

One of the girls in my group (who isn't a nice girl) started to put two and two together. She found the IP address. She exposed it in a really nasty way at school. She did it in the public gazebo at school in a really loud voice so everyone could hear. The girl cried and walked away. She didn't try and defend herself.

Her reputation has settled now. It was at the beginning at the year and it is June now. She lost a lot of trust from a lot of people for a while. I think she lost a lot of friends too. She seems happy again now. She's smiling more.

Fake Profiles and IP Addresses

Cyber safety experts rightly reinforce a consistent message: the internet is a public domain. As young people are acutely aware of this, many have fake accounts – not necessarily to do anything dodgy, but commonly to comment and follow pages and people anonymously. When young people digitally self-harm they usually use an existing fake account, or they set up a new fake account.

Unfortunately, many young people are not aware of how easy it is for their identity to be 'exposed' using an IP tracker. If young people can prove that two or more accounts involved in digital self-harm (one real profile and one or more anonymous profiles) have the same IP address/addresses, they can prove that it is probably the same person posting from both accounts.

The skill level that it takes to digitally self-harm is completely different from the skill level that it takes to track someone's IP address. Some young people are made vulnerable by their peers' technical skills.

'At my school I know kids use a website to track IP addresses,' said Regan. 'I'm not sure how to do it. I have never seen it or done it myself, but I have heard about it. Heaps of people have.' She continues, 'When friends are going well you don't assume that people are going to stoop to that level and expose you ... but it happens. You might expect your enemies to expose you, but you often find it is your *friends* that expose digital self-harm.'

Young people introduced me to a website they use to track IP addresses. The website allows a person to create a link to a supposedly innocent website, which is sent to the possibly self-harming person, usually via direct message to their real and/or fake account/s, enticing them to click on it. Once clicked, the person who sent it can view the IP address/es and see if the various IP addresses match.

Jane Webber from Code9 Parent, who offers cyber education for parents, shared her thoughts about the sneakiness involved in IP tracking. What she and I were both blown away by was the level of manipulation that it would take to get a young person to click on the link. Webber says, 'This is classic teenage manipulation. They would have to build trust and use deliberate tactics. This is click bait at its worst. Even if a young person receiving the link is thinking, "I shouldn't click on that link", chances are the fear of missing out would be too much for them to resist it.'

Real Concerns

One mother told me that her daughter heard about tracking IP addresses from an American television show called *iCarly*. It probably would have been one line in a whole show, but that was what took her interest! From there she googled it and then experimented with tracking IP addresses. What concerns me is that young people may only have a tiny amount of knowledge and no idea of what they are playing with. They may think they have the skills, but only have part of the information.

'I don't think young people fully think this stuff through,' says Webber. 'Kids may not be aware of how inaccurate IP tracking can be. The young person needs to be logged into both accounts at the time that someone is trying to track them. Young people may not fully understand what they are playing with. It is really easy to make a mistake when tracking an IP address and falsely accuse someone. That has massive knock-on effect socially.'

Webber also says, 'The other thing is that you aren't looking for the numbers to be the exactly the same. The last number can be different, which indicates it is a different device on the same network. It is the core numbers which need to be the same. They aren't breaking any laws. You can't find out that is it Annie Smith who lives in Stafford, but you can compare the IP address to as many accounts and comments that you suspect are theirs.'

Bottom line is, this is a pretty elaborate con job. This is scamming people. Young people have to be pretty tech savvy to be able to find out people's IP address. The whole thing could go 'boom' if a parent on the other end was disgruntled and went to the police or, worse still, an already unstable young person committed suicide after the additional pressure of being tracked.

Are you Ever Anonymous?

Whether it is possible to remain anonymous online was a question I raised during my interviews. The thought that a tech savvy young person who was not stable could easily conceal digital self-harm online was very frightening to me.

To understand internet privacy better, I spoke to Rob Micklewright, IT expert and Director of Request Technology. Micklewright has worked in the tech space for 20 years, and has helped me on many, many occasions to understand the changing landscape that young people are experiencing online.

'It is not that hard to be anonymous online,' explained Micklewright. 'It used to be more complex, but it isn't any more. The internet is a big world and for kids it can be pretty dangerous. However, the internet is still a public domain, even though there are ways to make yourself more private whilst using it. Without concealing your identity, nothing is private. Even when concealing it, you cannot assume privacy. There are obviously different levels of concealing your identity and different skills required to increase the level of privacy you want to achieve.

'Many years ago, privacy options were only accessible by tech geniuses. These days there are a number of ways that everyday people attempt to conceal their identity – setting up a fake account being the least effective. These "user friendly" ways are accessible to young people and could further enhance their ability to remain anonymous when digitally self-harming. Today, there are many ways of protecting your identity and privacy online, including proxy servers like "tor" and "onion routing". These days, VPN's (Virtual Private Networks) have become the most popular.'

What is a Virtual Private Network?

A VPN service can be downloaded from an app store, usually free, especially if you are not downloading much content. After confirming user requirements and the country that you want to connect to, the app then connects the device securely to another network through a VPN connection. This gives the device an IP address from the chosen country and network, meaning your device will show that it is being used from whichever country you choose to log into.

Many everyday people use VPN to access worldwide content. For example, during the London Olympics, people used VPN worldwide to access sports being played on English websites, as their country may have had limited coverage. It was a technically illegal but arguably very petty crime. Other reasons for using a VPN might be bypassing geographical restrictions on websites, watching streaming media like Netflix and Hulu in a different country that has more content, protecting yourself from snooping on untrustworthy WiFi hotspots, gaining some autonomy online by hiding your true location, protecting yourself from being logged while 'torrenting' (usually pirated content).

As you can see there are a few legitimate reasons to use VPN's, but probably not many for young people except for online streaming of movies from other countries or purchases from other countries. The reality is that VPN's also allow young people to hide destructive behaviour. They could also be using it to conceal their identity to comment without being recognised, bully someone, view pornography, digitally self-harm or visit any other website or content that their parents or school may not approve of.

Consider also the research on terrorism, weaponry, drugs and cults: dark stuff. VPN's play a big role in scams and criminal activity. 'That is why scams have been become so prevalent,' says Rob Micklewright. 'Many of my clients have been sent emails from scammers. They make it look legitimate but if you try to find where these scam emails have come from, they almost nearly always have been sent by someone connected to a VPN, using a fake email address, and that is where the trace ends. It's a rabbit warren from there. You can't even find out where in the world they are. It's often impossible for ACORN (Australian Cybercrime Online Reporting Network) to track.'

A VPN makes a complex trail that is difficult (often impossible) to track back to the original device, but it also tells people that there was a reason someone wanted to conceal that identity. 'If it was a matter of national security, and given enough resources, I am sure a lot of times people can be/have been tracked and caught,' added Micklewright. 'But also given a lot of resources and planning, people have been able to make things virtually untraceable.'

Young people could use a VPN to make it difficult to trace a fake profile or comment back to their IP address, hoping to further protect their privacy. However, Micklewright does caution,

'Young people still need to understand that a VPN flags them as doing something they want to keep hidden.'

What This Means for Parents, Schools and Professionals

I personally think there are many times young people know that their behaviour doesn't warrant the resources it would take for the police or school to track them. They also know there are school privacy policies in place that restrict them from exploring things further. They also know the limited knowledge that their parents have!

Carl Hotko, high school e-safety officer, explains, 'I don't think kids ever think they will get caught. Even if they do, they deny it, which then puts it back on the school to investigate. We can do what we can as a school but there are limitations. This is what makes digital self-harm really difficult to deal with on a school level. I don't know where we would ethically stand tracking an IP address but it would be tempting sometimes.'

Privacy legislation makes IP tracking of students problematic both legally and ethically. From a pastoral care perspective, trust is incredibly important and also incredibly fragile. Student support staff try not to do anything that would appear to break trust with students, or they may not come to us when they need help.

This issue of privacy is often why schools have opted for laptop leasing programs. Devices are owned by schools, leased by parents and used by students. Schools retain control of the software on the devices and also reinforce that nothing on the school-issued devices are actually private. This does not help schools monitor student or family-owned devices, but the school issued devices are more easily and ethically able to be monitored.

Hotko says, 'I think misuse in this space (which would warrant monitoring of usage or IP tracking etc.) is often difficult for schools to address. In our attempts to protect students (often from their own poor choices) we accept or try to deal inhouse with issues that in any other context may well become a police matter. Protecting a child from an outside predator is easy and clear-cut, but protecting our students from the consequences of their own actions is sometimes where our compassion gets in the way of justice or natural consequences.'

This is a story I was told by a young man who is now in university. The story doesn't involve digital self-harm, but shows how young people do track IP addresses, sometimes in desperation, to help their friends.

> I remember when we were in Year 8, one of the boys in our grade wanted to get another boy into trouble. He made a fake profile using the kid's name and photo. He then sent bullying messages from this account to his own account. The boy took screen shots of the messages and sent them to the teachers, trying to get this kid in trouble. The teachers all got involved. It was so intense and the

kid who he had tried to target was traumatised.

There was all this drama going on because the kid didn't do it, but the teachers believed he did. My friend was a tech genius and he said, 'Right, I am going to track the IP address and sort this out.' Once my friend found out that the IP address was the same as the boy who was claiming he was being bullied he went to the teachers. The teachers investigated it further. I don't know if they got the police involved but I think that it was just the IT guys. I'm not sure what happened but it all settled down.

Digital self-harm is a complex issue that is highly secretive and sensitive. Hotko says, 'The hidden nature of digital self-harm makes it really hard to predict and deal with. If we had a way of recognising it, we would have a better chance of preventing the catastrophic outcomes. The difficult part is going the next level and knowing what type of intervention is going to be most effective.'

I couldn't agree more.

Keeping an Open Mind

Parents have told me stories of children who have come to them in tears with elaborate stories of being 'punched' or 'kicked', when in fact the whole thing was fabricated. You can liken digital self-harm to an online version of a child claiming they were bitten, when they bit themselves.

This is one of the many complex stories that shows that digital self-harm is not just about 'bullying'. It reveals the intense and complex nature of digital self-harm that all professionals need to be aware of.

Tara's Story

Many times schools have spoken to me about specific students that they were struggling to successfully connect with and support. Tara was one of those students. Her teachers felt like they were constantly 'missing something', until the truth was discovered. Here is her story:

Tara was a competitive, national athlete who had a strong vision for her life. She trained hard and was very focused on her sport. Unfortunately, she also struggled with complex family issues that remained unresolved, regardless of the support provided. In Year 10 she left home and went to live with another family who offered to take her in.

Tara would self-harm her thighs and stomach regularly, taking to her skin with a blade. She often showed her friends, who would then report it to the guidance officer. Tara would sometimes claim that the injuries were from her dad's belt buckle, while other times she would confess it was self-harm. There always seemed to be a complex web of lies surrounding Tara's injuries and it was difficult to distinguish when she was telling the truth.

Tara also began to show her friends streams of horrific, hate-filled Facebook messages, which she claimed were from her mum. There were over 60 messages in total. These messages said things like:

    i am going to fucking kill u
    i am going to run u off the cliff
    i hate u u fucking cunt
    u are a whore
    u are no daughter of mine
    next time i am going to see you i am going to kill u
    i am going to destroy everything u own
    kill your self

When Tara eventually showed the guidance officer the messages, they were reported to the police. The whole story became very puzzling, as her parents denied sending them and there was no evidence on their phones. It was at that time that the head of school started to look at the structure of the language and question whether Tara had sent them to herself.

One of the police officers tracked the IP addresses and found that they were sent from Tara's computer. None of the students ever found out it was her, as the school tried to protect her reputation.

Tara was known to be a very troubled girl for whom self-harm was a big part of life. The guidance officer commented that the greatest self-harm Tara put herself through was training for her national competitions. It was beyond extreme. She wasn't eating correctly and she was often dehydrated. She trained every spare moment.

A Parent's Response

Parents need to be open to the possibility that online bullying could be generated by their own young person and be aware of the rising trend of digital self-harm. Unfortunately, they may never actually know the truth about digital self-harm, unless a young person chooses to confess their actions. If a parent finds out that a child they thought was being bullied was in fact bullying themselves, it can be a confusing and confronting reality.

One of the senior, experienced psychologists I employed many years ago sat me down to share his thoughts about one of the young people I was mentoring. He said this to me: 'Michelle, secrets that need to come to the surface usually do. If you stay closed enough for long enough, what is dark becomes light.' I have always remembered that. That day I had to choose to confront a huge number of lies surrounding this young person, or walk beside her until she was ready to talk. On reflection, I am glad I chose the latter.

Creating a safe space for communication of such a complex issue is not easy. It can be really frustrating. Accessibility, patience and willingness to take care of their needs regardless of how open they are prepared to be is what I would suggest. Pushing confessions is rarely helpful and may only add shame. Please refer to Chapter 5 for the discussion on Must-Have Conversations about self-harm, all of which stand true for digital self-harm.

Dr Hinduja wisely adds, 'Parents, educators, and youth-serving adults must also recognise that occasionally, the target and the aggressor are the same, and be sensitive and gracious while they investigate the matter – while also providing social support (and perhaps facilitating clinical support). I'd encourage those adults to also encourage the kids and teens in their lives to always know that they are there to serve as a listening ear without judgment or criticism ... and discuss healthier and more constructive ways to meet the deep-seated emotional needs their actions betray. Also, we know that youth sometimes confide in friends about suicidal ideation and their self-harming practices; we need to make sure we are discussing this phenomenon among adolescents so that they can understand its reality and offer support if someone in their peer group opens up to them.'

A Story of Connection

Karley started to encounter bullying. Social media was always at the centre of it. Kids from the outer circle of her friendship group would play nasty games, naming Karley as 'the most unliked person in the group'. Conversations where nasty comments were being made about her were 'screen-shot' and revealed to Karley. Through all this Karley still didn't return to self-harming. We talked about all of these and I always ensured Karley felt listened to and safe.

A few months later a message to Karley from 'do not follow private account closed' came through her Snapchat account. It touched on matters we felt only Karley or people close to Karley would possibly know about. It also made a clear directive of 'hurry up and kill yourself'.

Her parents and I first thought was some very disturbed girl had sent this message to Karley. We spoke with the school and we all shared serious concern for whoever was the writer of this message. Without ever hearing from Karley's mouth, we strongly believe Karley sent this message to herself. We still to this day don't know why she did this form of digital self-harm. We didn't question Karley over it;

we just took on the approach of 'soft and close'.

Whatever was going on with Karley, it was deep. She was hurting and she wanted everyone to know without actually saying it. Everyone at school knew about it, but no one said anything. From this, a beautiful relationship between Karley and myself has emerged. A shift has happened where I am now the safest, truest and softest place for Karley to fall into.

I am truly hesitant to suggest a blanket approach to communicating to young people about digital self-harm. My experience this year as shown me that each case is unique, and I feel that there are not enough research or case studies to provide concrete answers. However, I have found understanding of motives for digital self-harm and utilising these in initial discussions very helpful.

As with traditional self-harm, it is the approach which is important rather than the method. The right help at the wrong time is the *wrong* help. I spoke with Karley's parents about this incident, and we both decided to keep a close eye on her and increase support. The motive for digital self-harm could only be guessed as needing additional reassurance and attention during that period of her life.

In many other cases, direct and open conversations are important – especially if the behaviour is ongoing – as may be professional support and management of their online activity. All this has been discussed in previous chapters.

I continue to urge parents of pre-teens to set up social media to withstand the rockiest of the teenage years and stay connected to how they are handling their online reputations. This type of behaviour can escalate very quickly and cause any young person a great amount of guilt and shame, as well as a damaged social reputation.

Because of the short-lived nature of much digital self-harm, whatever intervention is chosen needs to be implemented immediately. Parents also need to focus on the underlying issues to ensure digital self-harm or other destructive behaviours do not keep resurfacing.

Warning Signs

Sadly, digital self-harm has been difficult for parents and educators to identify until it is too late. Here are some of the warning signs to look out for:
- Change in sleep or eating habits
- Lack of interest in social activities
- Withdrawal from friends and family
- Drop in grades at school
- Sadness or anxiety
- Agitation when receiving texts or notifications
- Inability to detach from devices
- Change to routine – like going to sleep later or waking up earlier
- Internet activity through the night
- Spending free time isolated or in their bedroom
- Bullying at school or friendship dramas
- Talk that they don't want to live

Concluding Thoughts

The complex topic of digital self-harm is a form of self-bullying that everyone needs to be aware of. However difficult these issues are to navigate, the base line answers are still the same: communication and connection. The next few chapters are dedicated to all these things.

Key Insights from this Chapter

- Digital self-harm is a relatively new phenomenon about which there is little public awareness.
- Digital self-harm is known as the online variant of self-harm. It is also called self-cyberbullying, cyber self-harm or self-trolling. Digital self-harm is the posting or sharing of demeaning information about oneself anonymously online.
- Times have changed, with online options for processing pain becoming a reality, but the base line drivers of human nature haven't. What motivates self-harm

and digital self-harm are closely linked.
- Young people who digitally self-harm can be exposed if someone tracks their IP address.
- The skill level that it takes to digitally self-harm is completely different from the skill level that it takes to track someone's IP address. Some young people are made vulnerable by their peers' technical skills.
- Parents need to be open to the possibility that online bullying could be generated by their own young person and be aware of the rising trend of digital self-harm. If a parent finds out that a child they thought was being bullied, was in fact bullying themselves, it can be both a confusing and confronting reality.

5

Must-Have Conversations

I have spent a great deal of time speaking to young people about why they find it so hard to speak to caring adults about self-harm. Young people have told me that they struggle to reveal self-harm for a range of reasons, including feeling embarrassed, ashamed, or afraid that their parents will try and stop them from hurting themselves. They also talked about the fear they had of their parents not understanding and getting angry with them.

Self-harm is something that is very difficult for caring adults to comprehend. It is also difficult for young people to explain, which makes initial conversations very hard. Louise Klar, student counsellor who has been working with self-harmers for more than a decade, says, 'Young people fear getting into trouble. That stops them from talking about what is happening and how they are feeling. If they thought that they would be met with compassion and understanding they would welcome the conversation.'

As I spoke to parents, they admitted that anger was an emotion they struggled with, especially when they felt they had been lied to or manipulated.

This is how Jane, Darcy's mother, explained her journey:

> Talking with Darcy about why she was self-harming seemed to evoke so much anger within me. She was upfront enough to say that it was because she was trying to get the message across to us that she was unhappy at the current school and wanted to change to the state high school. I was so angry to hear this! How could she be so emotionally manipulative? Why use such extreme behaviour to try and force our hand into giving her what she wanted? We'd had to deal with so many 'performances', lies and drama from Darcy that there was a harsh lack of compassion. The very fact that I felt like this towards my own daughter created

such internal turmoil for myself. I kept any of my own feelings to myself and didn't express anything to Darcy.

I wonder if this is why young people put self-harm on the internet before telling their parents. They know their friends aren't going to get angry with them. It feels like a safe place. I think they know it will leak out from there and eventually adults will find out. It feels less scary for their parents to hear secondhand.

The Royal College of Psychiatrists says that a person is more likely to self-harm if they feel people don't listen to them, that life is hopeless, that they are isolated and alone, that things are out of control or they are powerless. A lack of connection with caring adults is a key contributing factor for ongoing self-harm. This being said, I have also seen young people surrounded by the most caring and engaging family still struggle with self-harm. This may be due to the number of other risk factors or influences connected to their lives.

Rachael Rubio, student counsellor and a former teenage self-harmer, also shed some light on her parents' first reactions to self-harm. Part of her current job as a student counsellor is to notify parents that their child is self-harming. I asked her if she had any specific advice which would help parents handle those initial moments well.

Rubio says, 'Young people already feel so much guilt and shame around their behaviour. When parents hear that their child is self-harming, they ask themselves, *What have I done* or *what haven't I done?* They start looking for someone to blame. They start reacting out of a place of guilt and shame. It's easy for the whole conversation to go pear-shaped.'

The questions she wants parents to ask themselves is this: *How can I sit and be with my child and completely take the guilt and shame out of that moment?* We have to understand that that first moment – that first reaction – is critical to how the rest of the journey will go. The challenge is to not blame anyone or anything.

First Reactions

Regardless of whether a parent finds out about self-harm through a teacher, family friend, sibling or by snooping, it is usually a shock to them. Anne Ferrey describes it like this: 'Parents perception of family functioning are reported to be more positive than those of their children, and a large proportion of parents are unaware that their child has been self-harming. They are shocked when they find out. 'Other research describes parents' initial feelings as shock, anger and disbelief. In order to come to term with self-harm, the parents must work through these initial feelings.

When I asked parents how they initially felt when they found out that their son or daughter was self-harming, these are their replies:
- 'I felt sick to my stomach, and then I just felt numb. I didn't know what I had done wrong,' said Patricia.
- 'I was filled with every emotion you could think of at the same time,' said Tamika.

- 'At first I was worried; my thoughts went straight into picturing deep slices in her skin and the horrible emotional and mental place she must be in to want to do that to herself. I didn't understand cutting, why she was doing it, what was she getting out of doing it,' said Cathi.
- 'I suppose I turned on myself. How could I have failed my daughter so much as a mum to let her get to a place of thinking self-harming was way to solve a problem? We knew we were losing our little girl to something but didn't know to what,' said Laura.

It's a big call to ask parents to stay calm and collected during such an emotional time. The greatest advice I can give parents is to talk to a psychologist, counsellor or family friend before they speak to their young person. In my opinion, that is the wisest thing a parent could ever do. I can't say this enough—process your emotions away from your young person.

Collett Smart, psychologist and teacher with more than 20 years' experience working with young people, wisely adds, 'I strongly recommend that both dads and mums have support. As a couple, through a counsellor, and also through a close friend or family member, apart from their partner. Someone who is not as emotionally involved with the situation. It's important to have times where you can have a mental and physical break from the family trauma or pain. This is not a form of "escape" – it's a form of self-care. Self-care is vital to your own health and strength. Fill your cup, because an empty cup has nothing to give others.'

Starting a Conversation

Talking to young people about self-harm may seem daunting to parents, but young people want you to approach this challenging topic with confidence. As this statement from Eunice below indicates, you can get mixed messages from young people about their readiness to talk about self-harm. On one hand they may look like they don't want to talk, but on the other hand they are wishing for their parents to dig deep and enquire about their state of mind.

She writes:

> Looking back on my days when my mental health was the lowest, I felt as if I needed something that I could lean on to help me cope. Unfortunately for me, when I was 13 I came to believe that my crutch should be self-harm. I battled with self-harm for about four years. At first it had been my last resort to cope and then it became something I went to straight away. I struggled with a lot of changes in high school, and with friendships and eventually family sickness and my dad's death. The thing about self-harming is that I felt so incredibly shameful of what I had done. I blocked them out, but yet I wanted people who cared about me to see, or to dig, to ask if I was okay.

Any conversation about self-harm needs to be approached carefully, with genuine empathy. I talk about the concept 'soft and close' a lot in my work. I can't say those two words enough as I start this conversation with you! When in doubt, always resort back to 'soft and close' – meaning your body language, tone of voice and your actual words should resemble all of those things!

Be aware of things that disconnect people. Judgements, criticisms, overreactions, control, insensitivity and a lack of knowledge amongst other things will impact conversations negatively. Avoid these like the plague. None of these are 'soft and close'.

Specific lines that I recommend parents avoid include:
- There must be something wrong with you for you to do this
- I think you are doing this to get attention
- If you don't stop I will have to punish you
- Lots of people go through bad stuff in life and don't end up cutting
- You will end up in hospital or worse
- Tell me where you are hiding your blades now
- How long has this been going on?
- I know how you feel

- I bet your friends are doing it and that's why you started
- Why do you want to kill yourself?

Winging conversations of significance is never a good idea. Come prepared with a road map but hold your plans lightly. Your teenager may take the conversation in an entirely different direction. Your road map starts with an introduction, a series of questions or thoughts that guide the conversation, and then has an ending. The right landing is critical.

Your Road Map – Nailing the Introduction

I can't tell you how many times I have seen a parent turn a bad day into a disaster by wading into an intense discussion without preparing their son or daughter well. I suggest you start by giving some warning that the conversation is going to happen. Don't just spring it on them in the car, or while you are shopping or cooking dinner. I would prefer you say, 'I need to have an important conversation with you. It is going to take about 45 minutes. Would you like to walk and talk or sit in your bedroom?' Choose your time and location carefully.

They need to know you will shut up at some point! That is why you need to tell them how long it will take. If it's open-ended it might feel too overwhelming for them to handle. If the conversation goes longer, great – but at least they don't feel like you are going to trap them all night!

In saying that, I have a recommendation. Don't let the conversation go longer than you both can emotionally handle. Conversations that last longer than an hour tend to lose their quality. In my opinion, shorter, more focused conversations leave young people coming back for more. I would rather have regular shorter conversations than longer conversations that leave everyone emotionally exhausted.

Boys and girls may have different communication preferences. If you have a son, you might find that less eye contact and more physical movement while talking may induce better communication. If you have a daughter, the closer physical proximity and more eye contact the better. Think of two women in a coffee shop chatting about life's issues. A lot of backstabbing happens behind women's backs, so face to face is reassuring to girls. Boys, on the other hand, find direct eye contact quite confrontational and threatening, so walking and talking, or driving and talking, might be a better fit for them.

Your Road Map – Navigating the Conversation

This may sound crazy but please think of this as your golden opportunity to build trust and connection with your child. You may never get this opportunity again. In fact, I really hope you don't get an opportunity exactly like this again! There may never be another time when they are so vulnerable and need you in such a specific way. Handle it with care, realising that each word will make an impact.

Try to create a safe, supportive and non-judgemental environment that reinforces what is healthy and true, while leaving room to understand a young person's current state of mind. Never assume what they are thinking. Always ask, even if you think you might not like the answer. You will need your poker face at times. A few awkward pauses are okay. If they don't want to answer, remember this: be content to not know. It won't necessarily change the way you parent.

Reassure your child that you don't think they are a failure because they are having difficulties. Some of the most brilliant minds in the world had moments of significant struggle. I don't think you can reassure them of this enough. This may be the first time in their lives they have felt such deep and overwhelming emotions, and they don't yet have the maturity to know that people can get through such times.

Here are some thoughts and questions that might help you frame and guide the conversation:
- My greatest focus and concern is supporting you the best way I can. This conversation is about helping me do that.

- Is there anything I could do that would make a difference?
- I need you to help me understand self-harm. How does self-harm make you feel better?
- What time of day are you struggling the most? What can we do as a family to help you at that time?
- How well are you sleeping?
- Would seeing a doctor be something you were open to?
- What is it like talking to me about self-harm? Who else are you talking to?
- There are some things that I need to talk to you about for your safety. Would you be happy to talk about some of these practical things with me? I need you to reassure me that you are safe, and we need to keep these lines of communication open.
- What positives can we add to your life now? Is there anything that you are missing out on that you used to love doing?
- At your worst points, how bad are your feeling? If you don't have

words to describe it, could you give me a rating out of 10?
- How are your friendships and relationships going?

How are you feeling about your relationships with each of us in the family right now?
- Is there anything that is really concerning you right now that I can help you with?
- Is there anything you can't talk to me about that you might want to talk to someone else about? I can arrange that for you.
- If you ever want to text me instead of talking to me, you know my number!

Your Road Map – Landing the Conversation

Once you start the conversation, realise your child may repeat every word you say over and over in their head for days to come. For that reason, please don't let it be the last time you talk as they will need to clarify things that you have said. My guess is that they will misinterpret some of what you have said if left as a solo conversation. I would suggest that you check in and keep checking in every few days.

You might land your conversation by saying, 'This is not the last time I want us to talk. How about I check in with you in a few days, or if you want to talk to me earlier I am always here to talk. The most important thing for you to know is that I love you and there is nothing I won't do for you. There is nothing we can't get through when we love each other.'

Darcey's Story

I don't think I have met a parent alive that felt like they got their first conversation about self-harm right. And let me reassure you of this. I don't think that your young person expects you to. What they want most of all from you is a *feeling.* They need to feel that you love and care about them. They need to feel that you have their best interests at heart. And the rest is just details. Details matter but nowhere near as much as the feeling. If your words are failing, fall back on feelings. *Feelings matter.*

Darcey was 16 years old when she came to see me. She was the perfect example of a young girl with many of the risk factors (anxiety, impulsivity, ongoing challenges socially, significant bullying). What she did have going for her was an engaged and loving family who went to great lengths to care and intervene. I wanted to include her story here, written in her words as it shows some of the warning signs that her family and coach noticed and some of the initial 'imperfect conversations' which kick-started her recovery.

Here is Darcey's story:

> At the end of Year 7 I had been struggling with friendships. I had been excluded from a lot of groups and it was affecting me. I had been bullied pretty badly. Sometimes it is hard to talk about things that are going on in your life. I find it hard to re-talk about things that have already happened. Bringing hurtful things back up are difficult because you want to move on from them.

When you first get approached by someone who asks, 'Are you self-harming?' it is a bit of a weird conversation. It is a bit of a worry because you don't think people know. All of a sudden you feel like people are taking away something that you thought was helping you, and you are losing a coping strategy.

The first person who talked to me about it was my older sister. She was getting suspicious of things. We would go out in summer and I didn't want to wear shorts. The moment I was out of the water I had a towel on me. That was what gave it away to her. At the time we had friends who had a boat. I was always self-conscious. When I was getting changed, or when she came into a room all of a sudden, I was really uncomfortable with her being there. That was weird for me because I used to not worry about her seeing me half naked! The fact that I was sad, and not acting like myself was unusual for me. My personality was usually loud. She was watching how I was handling things in life. She asked me, 'Are you self-harming?' I said, 'No.' She didn't ask again. She didn't want to push it.

The second person was my coach at gymnastics. I don't know how she knew. Looking back, it might have been because she saw marks on my body but I can't be sure because she never said. She came to me after class one day. She said, 'How are you going? How is everything at school? How are the girls?' I said, 'Everything is fine.' Then she said, 'Are you self-harming?'

I said, 'No.'

She said, 'Good.' And then she didn't say anything else again.

The third people were my parents. Another gymnastics coach saw my self-harm on my thighs. Then she went to talk to my parents about it. I didn't know but my sister had also talked to my parents about it.

My parents talked to me that night. They asked me if I could show them the cuts on my thighs. That was really daunting. For me I didn't ever really fully understand why I was doing it, so it was really hard to explain to someone else. It was hard to re-explain to them. Dad was angry and upset and was trying to get me to tell him why I was cutting. Mum was crying a lot and in shock. She didn't know what to do. I think they were hoping I would know what to do next.

The reason why I started cutting was because I saw a girl next to me in class who had cuts all up and down her thighs. I didn't even know the girl. They were drawings of things and names of people. I asked her why she did it and she said, 'I get bored and I get my protractor and I draw up and down my legs.' That was literally all it was. I was vulnerable right then and it stuck in my head. It wasn't the internet or a big discussion with anyone.

I was going through a hard time in high school and I was looking for something to help. I thought it might help. I self-harmed from Year 7 to Year 8 when mum took me to get some help. Getting help worked for me. It was knowing that there was a different way to get everything out. It also helped that there was someone else to talk to, besides just my mum and dad.

Looking back with an older mentality, I don't think that what I was doing was warranted. I think it was really dumb. I wanted it to be a release and keep my mind off my problems. I need my mind to be active. I still do. When I have nothing on my mind that is when my thoughts get the better of me. I hope this helps someone. Xx

Jacob's Story

Boys also vividly recall the first time someone discussed self-harm with them. Many of them could describe the person, place and exact words that were exchanged. I met Jacob in his late teens, but by this time he could name several people who had cared enough to start meaningful conversations with him. Jacob's story reminds me of the lasting impact caring adults can make.

I was about 14 when I started cutting, and about 16–17 when I started having trouble with my weight. Would eat only a few things a day and my weight dropped significantly, down into the 60s[kg] if I remember correctly.

I was cutting mainly, little bit of starving myself a few times and neglecting my diabetes to dangerous points. At one point I was cutting almost religiously daily, mainly on my upper leg. When I was admitted to hospital, if I was having a bad day, I'd cut up my arm lightly all over. Three times I've OD'd on prescribed medication (insulin) as part of a suicide attempt and the third time I cut quite a lot of my forearm and upper leg.

I've been living with depression/anxiety for about five or six years now, so it's hard to remember names and places when it all started happening. I didn't really know what was going on with me. All I knew was I started hating school, bullying was coming and going and I was still grasping my parents' divorce. I was terrified of school and had started self-harming.

It wasn't until I had a breakdown in the car before school that my mother suggested that I might have depression. We went from psychologist to psychologist until we met one that I really related to.

A woman named 'Vikki' from my Diabetes Clinic gave me the basics like 'fight or flight'. I didn't start to really understand what was going on until I went to a psychologist. Before that I didn't really have anyone to talk to about mental health.

I can't speak for all boys/men, but it was very hard to talk about: to this day I struggle to talk to my psychiatrist about it. As blokes, we're supposed to be tough and not show weakness. We're supposed to just take hits on the chin and walk along like nothing is wrong. If we say we're scared or uncomfortable or just flat out depressed, we're told to take a teaspoon of cement and toughen up. My father still doesn't understand how to go about it all and a lot of my male classmates don't either. There is definitely a stigma about it which I do try to break.

Minimise Vulnerability

The key to opening communication with our sons or daughters is providing them with an environment that makes them feel safe, whatever that environment is. Our job as parents is to try and minimise vulnerability, and not make communication a 'pressure point'. Only then will they express how they really feel without fear of being shamed or criticised. Pushing visits to psychologists may not help but only make communicating feel more daunting if done the wrong way.

Simple tricks, like ensuring conversations with boys are best back-dropped by another activity (like driving or walking), is something that some parents use. Not only does it appeal to their biological strength as a male, it also ensures boys don't feel like they are being interviewed. The moment they feel that they are the centre of attention with spotlights on them, it creates a feeling of vulnerability and they clam up.

I recommend focusing conversations on topics that are of interest to them, or topics they have confidence in talking about. Find common ground and build a bond with them that doesn't make them feel like your 'project'. Talk about topics that they are more knowledgeable than you in, as it makes them feel like they have something worthwhile to contribute. This builds their confidence and will more likely make way for further communication.

When you begin a difficult conversation, don't start with the most difficult material. They will instantly feel overwhelmed and out of their depth. Always begin a conversation with something that makes them feel assured and secure. Ask simple questions that they know how to answer with ease before asking more complex questions.

Recognise when you are pushing them to communicate outside of their comfort zone. If it isn't flowing naturally, step back and leave it alone. There are times when you have to be content not to know how they feel until they are ready to talk to you about it. Pushing conversations makes boys feel out of control and uncomfortable. It never brings out the best in them.

Try and talk to your son alone when there is no audience. Keep onlookers to a minimum. I knew a boy who had something important to talk to his parents about, but instead of talking to two parents at once he asked his mother to leave the room.

'I know Dad will tell you later,' he said, 'but I would rather handle one of you at a time.' This was about all the vulnerability he could cope with.

Remember too that boys understand logic. They need fair boundaries and absolutes that make sense. Too much uncertainty and indecision and they get lost. They don't stand well on shifting sand. Say less and be clear about what you say.

Keep it simple. Keep it clear. Keep it honest and real.

The Temptation to Snoop

I recently received this question from a mum who found herself in a dilemma after snooping: 'I read my daughter's journal a few days ago, and I found out that she was self-harming. I was SO SHOCKED!!! She has been using my nail scissors in the bathroom which always go missing. Do I tell her that I read her journal and break her trust? How do I approach this?'

Mums usually go looking for information on their teenager's phone or journal when they know that something isn't right. They know they shouldn't snoop, but curiosity and concern get the better of them. They are always well intended, but often a little misdirected. We think the discovery is going to help us parent our child, but all it does is load us up with an extra dilemma to deal with. If mums would just listen and trust their gut instincts, they wouldn't have to snoop!

I suggest that we be content to 'intuitively know' without knowing all the facts. The interesting thing is that knowing the facts doesn't usually change the way we parent our kids. What it does do is give us the confidence (or ammunition) to do exactly what we thought we should be doing in the first place. So, what are we really doing? We are hunting for validation. If we would only validate ourselves by reassuring ourselves that our gut instincts are likely right, we wouldn't have to break young people's trust.

Once we have snooped we can't un-see what we have just seen so we now have a dilemma. A parent's knee-jerk reaction may be to immediately confront their son or daughter with their discovery. However, I encourage you to give it a few days and then decide objectively what is the best for them.

You might feel a range of emotions including anger, sadness, frustration, helplessness, shame, guilt or even disgust. It is normal to feel strong emotions, but you need to be careful not to misdirect them towards your son or daughter. Focus on being the parent, and if that means holding off telling them, do that. Secrets aren't good for relationships, but neither is adding stress on top of a stressful or delicate situation. Please play the smart card rather than the emotional card.

There are times when direct conversations about self-harm are not only important, but critical. Young people are often waiting for parents to wade into their world with honesty, showing that they are not blind or ignorant to their situation. Conversations that move things forward in a positive direction are powerful when done well.

There are also times when young people aren't ready to talk about it. If you don't feel they are ready to talk, don't push a confession. Any time I have worked with mild self-harmers I have always ignored the self-harm itself unless a young person has wanted to talk about it. Why? I recognise that self-harm is often clouded with secrecy and shame and that pushing conversations is not often useful.

That means, if you find a razor in your daughter's room with dry blood on it or you are concerned about your son's reckless concern for his safety, you may be better having a conversation about their mood or wellbeing rather than the razor you found or the bruise you saw. Don't ignore your young person's mental health but be smart about how you approach it.

A simple conversation about your concern that starts with any one of these lines may be all it takes to open up communication:

- I am concerned about you
- I want you to know that I am here if you want to talk
- If you want to talk to anyone, even if it's not me, I will organise that for you
- How can I best support you right now?

You may have to offer this support over and over, but if you keep offering it, chances are that one day your young person will take you up on it. The alternative of coming in with 'all guns blazing' is likely to be counter-productive, and will possibly even backfire.

'Soft and close', parents! My advice is always: 'soft and close'.

Concluding Thoughts

Research is clear that repeat self-harm is common, and therefore it is important to address self-harm as early as possible. Self-harm is also linked to serious health issues and therefore is something that we need to treat with care. I want to clarify that throughout this chapter I am not suggesting that parents ignore findings of self-harm. I am suggesting that it is *how* parents *address* self-harm that will make all the difference. The next chapter will help you talk to your young person about seeing a professional or other support people outside of the family.

Key Insights from this Chapter

- Self-harm is something that is very difficult for caring adults to comprehend. It is also difficult for young people to explain, which makes initial conversations very hard.

- The question to ask yourself is this: How can I sit and be with my child and completely take the guilt and shame out of that moment?
- We have to understand that that first moment – that first reaction – is critical to how the rest of the journey will go. The challenge is to not blame anyone or anything.
- Any conversation about self-harm needs to be approached carefully, with genuine empathy.
- When in doubt, always resort back to 'soft and close' – meaning your body language, tone of voice and your actual words should resemble all of those things!
- Try to create a safe, supportive and non-judgemental environment that reinforces what is healthy and true, while leaving room to understand a young person's current state of mind.
- Never assume what a young person is thinking. Always ask, even if you think you might not like the answer. If they don't want to answer, remember this: be content to not

know. It won't necessarily change the way you parent.
- A few awkward pauses are okay.
- Reassure your child that you don't think they are a failure for having difficulties. Some of the most brilliant minds in the world had moments of significant struggle. I don't think you can reassure them of this enough.
- Keep it simple. Keep it clear. Keep it honest and real.

6

The Role of Professional Support and Schools

It is very common for young people to feel awkward or ashamed when their parents find out about self-harm. You have to initiate the discussion, but you may need to handball it to someone else to help out pretty quickly. A third party such as a psychologist, counsellor or mentor might be a good neutral person for a young person to talk to. They may even help your family keep open and honest communication going.

I would suggest parents always offer medical support to a young person who is self-harming and am surprised how many families try to handle things in-house. There are many perceptions of self-harm. Some see self-harm as normal development behaviour or, in other words, as 'teens just being dramatic teens'. Others attribute self-harm directly to mental health problems and therefore take more of a medical route when treating it. I have met others who see self-harm as a naughty, controlling or manipulative behaviour that needs to be disciplined or punished.

How a parent sees self-harm will greatly influence how they respond to self-harm, who they talk to about self-harm, and if and where they go to get support. The problem is that our perceptions as parents can be limited. The more we try and handle self-harm in-house, the higher risk we have of getting it wrong. There is safety in a multitude of professional and wise counsel.

One counsellor I spoke to said she has seen young people say, 'If you don't take me seriously I am going to do this more or I can be going to do this worse. I am going to show that this is not an attention-seeking behaviour and this is real for me.' I firmly believe that young people need the voice to determine what treatment is best for them, which includes medical support.

However, for many, getting young people to talk to a professional can be as difficult as 'selling ice to an Eskimo'. Evidence suggests that most young people are reluctant to access professional support for mental health problems. It's hard for young people to reach and build a relationship with someone new during a really vulnerable time. Parents need to realise how big a challenge they may be facing. Some of the mindsets that hinder young people from accessing a professional are that they don't want to talk to anyone, they don't think there is a problem, or they assume counselling won't help anyway.

It may help to take yourself back to being 14 years old again. Did you ever have a moment when you said to yourself, 'I don't know who I am. I don't know what I want. Everything is overwhelming to me right now'? That may be the place where your young person is when they are self-harming. Parents will be able to identify with some of those feelings. Everything is magnified where you are in that place and nothing makes sense. Parents may be the last people they want to listen to.

Listed below are some practical ways to introduce the idea of counselling to a young person who is self-harming. The same approach can be used to talk to them about seeing a doctor. One size does not fit all and therefore choosing the right tack is critical. Factors such as their age and your family dynamics may affect your approach.

Option 1: The Caring Approach
You might say, 'We are really concerned about you and we wouldn't be doing our job as your parents if we weren't going to get you some extra help.'

Option 2: Suggest a Trial Period
You might say, 'I really believe this can help. I want you to give this a go for three sessions and if you don't like it we can review it.'

Option 3: Tackle Things as a Family
You might say, 'This is a family issue that we all have to take responsibility for. We will be going and getting help as well. We might see another person, depending on what you are comfortable

with, but we will be a part of the process too.'

Option 4: Appeal to their Sense of Compassion
You might say, 'Would you go to counselling for me? Sometimes it is easier to do something for someone else rather than do it for yourself.'

Option 5: Simply be the Parent
You might say, 'There are some decisions we have to make as your parents. This is an adult decision that I need to make for you. I want you to trust that I know what is best for you.'

Option 6: Try to Normalise Therapy
You might say, 'Everyone needs support from time to time. It's actually really normal. Can I talk to you about some people I have known who have gone through tough times?'

Option 7: Give them Options
You might say, 'Check these websites out. Do any of these psychologists look like a good fit for you? Would you like me to make an appointment for you

or would you like to make an appointment for yourself? I'm happy to go with you or I can drop you off at the door?

Option 8: Leave the Door Open
You might say, 'I imagine this is difficult for you to talk about, but I want you to know that when you are ready I am here. I am also very happy for you to speak to a counsellor of your choice if talking to me is too difficult. You can text me if it is easier for you.'

There may be times when, despite your best efforts, young people may refuse to get support. If they won't come, I encourage you to go alone and start the journey by yourself.

The Difference Professionals Can Make

I have seen many parents emotionally withdraw after they have engaged a professional, feeling that they have done all they can do. However, I want to emphasise that a professional can't replace parents. You can't hand parenting over to anyone else. Please show up, in real life and counselling sessions, every time, whole heartedly.

This is a mother's story of how counselling and family support produced good results:

Our daughter was using scissors. Nothing sharp enough to slice, but she left marks that resembled shallow scratches on her upper thighs. Always out of sight. She did most of her harming while in the bathroom. It's the one place she knew no one would interrupt her.

The turnaround in relation to self-harming was seeing a counsellor. I know that seems simplistic, but they started talking each week and I think it was more the fact that Brianna finally felt heard.

We were listening, she had our attention. The reality of Brianna not coping hit us hard. Why did it take us so long to realise that her negative behaviours were a result of us not listening? Why did we choose to only see a 'bad' child and not a child crying for serious help!?

We didn't see a huge change in Brianna initially. Slowly over the months we started to see our usual beautiful, bubbly, confident and sassy girl emerge.

A Word About Boys

After all my talk about professional support I am going to whisper one word of caution: *we need to listen to young people.* I received a text message from a mum who wanted her son to see a counsellor. It read, 'My son is possibly looking at talking to someone about his stuff. I've been talking to him about seeing someone for a while, but he's resisted. Apparently, it's not a 'manly thing'. He's coming around now though...'

What made me smile was how desperate this mum was to persuade her son that counselling would help, based on the positive experience she had had talking to a trusted person. Her son was not convinced that having a spotlight on his emotions would be so helpful. I find that most mothers are convinced that if we can get our sons to communicate, they will feel so much better.

On average, Youth Excel's Psychology Clinic which I founded and managed, registered at least ten times more girls than boys. Research suggests that girls were twice as likely to use mental health services for support, with the stigma attached to mental illness being a particular threat to boys. Experience has taught me that many teenage boys (not all but many) have a pre-determined suspicion for counselling centres, whereas girls are more open to receiving an hour of someone's undivided attention.

If this sounds like your son, make sure you play to his strengths. Sitting in a room may not be his preferred method or communication or style. That is totally okay as long as he is finding ways to connect with caring adults who want to invest in his life.

When I asked author and educator Maggie Dent if counselling centres were the answer for boys she said, 'Seldom. A boy will only open up to someone he thinks likes him and he can trust. That can take a long time. Boys are incredibly private about personal things and don't want anyone else to know how screwed up they feel. If a boy's first attempt at getting help is unsatisfactory, they may never reach out again. Their fear of betrayal of trust and negative consequences of public knowledge of their vulnerability is paramount. When they have found a person they trust that really offers support in an adolescent-friendly way, they will refer other adolescents and they will turn up.'

Although we can't simplify gender differences in help seeking, we need to be aware of young people's desire to use different sources of help, knowledge of mental health problems and beliefs in the usefulness of help. Regardless of gender we need to listen to what is working or not working for them and why. Trust, rapport and a positive experience are huge factors in engaging any young person in therapeutic relationships.

Support Services to Consider

I have met many parents who have been told that their son or daughter is self-harming (by teachers or sports coaches) and walked away from initial conversations (sometimes even with a referral card in their hand) without any idea of what they wanted to do next. The shock of that conversation probably erased 90% of what was said. So here is a list of people you could contact for support. I always suggest a combination of formal and informal support.

Hospital or Ambulance – An ambulance or local hospital is the best place if you ever feel your young person is unsafe or threatening suicide or you are unable to care for wounds at home. Unfortunately, this is a very hard decision that parents sometimes have to make.

General Practitioner – GPs are always worthwhile to have on hand and are more accessible than specialists. In Australia, you will need to visit a GP in order to gain a referral to a specialist.

Ask for a longer appointment time with your doctor to gain this referral. If you don't have a family doctor, ask for a recommendation from your local school or friends. I would look for a doctor who frequently works with young people and has a special interest in mental health. I always recommend that parents make a personal appointment with the doctor of choice prior to taking the young person if they are under the age of 14. You may only get one shot at engaging them, so you want to make sure you get the best professional fit that you can.

Psychiatrist – A psychiatrist is a medical doctor who specialises in mental health. They specialise in diagnosing and treating people with mental illness and are authorised to prescribe medication. Some psychiatrists work with children and adolescents while others do not. This website will help: Royal Australian and New Zealand College of Psychiatry: www.ranzcp.org

Clinical and Counselling Psychologists – Psychologists are mental health experts who provide diagnosis and therapeutic treatment of mental illnesses. They are not authorised to prescribe medication. Psychologists usually have special areas of interest, so check out their profiles for a summary of their work experience. This website will help: Australian Psychological Association: www.psychology.org.au

Counsellors – Counsellors have various qualifications usually ranging from two to four years of study. They offer confidential communication about life issues in order to help solve problems and are usually great at listening, caring and working holistically with families. This website will help: Australian Counselling Association: www.theaca.net.au

Small Group Therapy – Some psychology, counselling and medical services offer small group support programs. Phoning their reception will provide you with information about their programs.

Life Coaching – Life coaches offer goal orientated support for young people. Some young people will be ready for this form of support and others may be better suited to psychologists and counsellors. Be careful to investigate the coach's qualifications and experience thoroughly, as regulations for this industry are limited. Used in conjunction with a GP, life coaches can provide a lot of positive benefits.

Youth Worker/Mentor – Your local government should be able to provide you with a list of local youth services in your area.

Teachers, School Counsellor and Chaplain – School support staff can provide young people with a familiar, trustworthy, accessible and free service. The down side is that many teachers, school counsellors and chaplains have limited time. Young people may need additional support.

Youth Pastors/Leader – Church youth groups are a low fee (or no fee) Friday night option for families. Young people have instant connection to older role models and positive values framed in a religious context.

Interest Groups – Sports, Dance, Art, Drama, Gaming, Chess and the like. If you have a child wanting to disconnect from sport or any other interest group, please try and keep them engaged. Push through! Keeping them positively active through the teen years is critical, especially if they hit a few bumps in the road. It is harder to get a stone moving once it is still.

Family Members and Friends – They may not have letters after their name, but they can be an incredible support. The best part is that young people may already trust them. That is the biggest plus. The down side is that confidentiality can be a concern for young people, which restricts them from really opening up. This is a tricky one to navigate as a family.

The Role of Schools

Schools play an integral role in identifying and supporting students who are self-harming. Teachers should recognise the amount of courage it takes for a young person to disclose self-harm. Self-harm is a powerful statement, and often is a cry for help. If teachers are in the box seat of identifying self-harm, they play a powerful role in young people's lives.

Their dealing with incidents of disclosure, as well as general communication about the topic, should be handled with care.

Each school has an internal referral system, which usually progresses from teaching staff through to school counsellors, then to parents and external referrals. While no system is perfect, I have found that every school has within it champions of young people's mental health. Young people naturally gravitate to these adults because they are more likely to feel understood and cared for.

Teachers, like parents, find self-harm confronting and may not always be educated in how to approach it or what to do. As a result, it is not uncommon for young people to have negative experiences involving teachers. Myths around self-harm often cloud teachers' interactions with students. Teachers may feel like self-harm exceeds their qualifications, capacity or interests as professionals.

However, a young person's mental health has a direct impact on learning, and teacher's classroom observations may be critical in identifying and supporting a young person. I would personally love to see fewer negative experiences for students who self-harm, and therefore advocate for more professional development for teachers.

Privacy Issues

Teachers are bound by code of conduct and policy. Students know if they talk to a teacher it will progress beyond that initial conversation to student support and parents. This often hinders young people from being honest and open with teachers who they may otherwise speak to.

Here are some guiding points for teachers.

Self-harm is an intensely private issue, which often needs to be dealt with in a system that demands communication between involved parties. Make appropriate in-school referrals based on factual information and/or 'gut feelings' in accordance with your school's policy and procedure.

Teachers should ensure that all conversations regarding self-harm or wellbeing are conducted in a private, non-judgemental way. Simple gestures like creating a context of privacy to talk to students of concern go a long way in protecting students. This can be challenging to create but needs to be a priority.

It is important to note that students who wish to discuss self-harm may 'test the waters' and slowly disclose information. It may therefore be necessary for teachers to document conversations and observations, whether that be through incident report forms or anecdotal notes.

I recommend that teachers do not ask other students to comment on their friend's mental health; neither should they go out of their way to engage in general discussions about a student. It is critical that teachers remain integral in protecting students' privacy.

Teachers should always exercise the same care for students who disclose friends' self-harming behaviour. Disclosures of this nature should be reported as per the school's policy and procedure.

It is critical that teachers keep students and parents notified of who needs to be communicated with regarding self-harm and that everyone involved hasa choice in this disclosure.

Communication between teaching staff needs to be handled with care. There is obviously no place for corridor conversations, judgements or gossip, and it is critical that teachers adhere to these practices to protect students.

Teachers should see themselves as a 'link in a chain of support' and suggest that students start a conversation with a school-based health care professional or external health care professionals.

It needs to be acknowledged that trust drives open conversations and therefore students often open up to the person they want help from. This can make transferring them to another professional tricky. Teachers should see their role as helping young people connect with the appropriate persons as well as providing them with ongoing support.

Parents should be notified once a disclosure is made or factual evidence of self-harm is gained, or at any time a school deems communication to be in a student's best interests.

Conversations with parents can be tricky if schools are the first to notify parents that self-harm is happening. They should be approached with factual evidence, reassurance of privacy policies, referrals to health care professionals and a lot of care. Denial may be parents' first reaction, so ongoing conversations may be necessary.

Displaying appropriate crisis numbers within the school makes it easier for students to find anonymous help.

Great teachers don't wipe their hands of things once a referral is successful. Checking in with students in the months and even years to follow is a powerful reinforcement that their ongoing journey is important. So is requesting that parents and guidance officers keep teachers updated with the students' progress and needs.

Teachers should be open to asking questions and getting support when they need it too. Dealing with students who self-harm can be complex, and there may be questions that arise about ethical practice, care and referrals that need to be made.

School-Based Warning Signs

A list of warning signs to identify self-harm has already been covered in Chapter 1. However, I have included some specific warning signs that are more likely to be seen within a school context. These are signs that teachers need to be aware of:
- Being absent from school without reason, or truanting
- Having unexplained marks on the body
- Not completing assignments or homework
- Wearing school jumpers or jackets in hot weather
- Wearing wide wrist bands that are never removed
- Being cautious or conscious of their body being touched
- Exhibiting social challenges or bullying

- Withdrawing from existing friendships
- Having low self-esteem or confidence
- Having sharp objects in their possession
- Possessing pencil sharpeners without blades in them
- Avoiding situations where arms and legs are showing eg. gymnastics or swimming carnivals
- Talking about self-harm or suicide

Identifying Self-Harm in Boys

Remember that it is a young person's *intention* that defines self-harm. Intentions can be difficult to 'read'. It can be hard for adults to tell the difference between normal boy behaviour and self-harm, and suspicions can't be confirmed with communication. Behaviour could easily be misinterpreted by onlooking adults as impulsive or immature. I therefore wonder how much self-harm remains unidentified, leaving young people unsupported.

Boys often use humour to deflect their inner thoughts and feelings. As an example, a teacher noticed a 'smiley' a boy had on his arm. He had used a cigarette lighter to burn his skin. When his teacher asked about it he said, 'I was just being silly.'

The boys were all joking about it and he was wearing it proudly. When his teacher talked to me about it he said, 'It is so hard to know whether boys are really in need or just mucking around. I'm concerned about that kid. As adults we could make so many assumptions and get it so wrong. Boys are conditioned to not need help and they always leave you second guessing.'

The Big Picture for School Counsellors

School counsellors also deal with the knock-on effect of self-harm on other students. Rachael Rubio, student counsellor and former self-hamer, says, 'We get a lot of parents calling the school stressed because their child has been acting out. It has come to their attention that one their child's friends has sent a graphic image of them self-harming. The child has been trying to help their friend and it's become too much for them. A really common situation is when they are sent an image, and try to text back, they can't get onto them. This really distresses them.'

As you can imagine this makes self-harm more complex an issue for them to deal with. Rubio continues, 'We have put a lot of time into helping young people know how to help their friends in these situations. They can't try and be their counsellor, psychologist or parent or sibling. They can't blur the lines. They have to realise they don't have to carry the responsibility to the level others do. They just have to do things that friends do and don't do things that psychologists do. Young people can carry a lot of guilt that they can't be and do more.

'One thing we have to do is debunk the myths. Some of the things that friends might tell a young person are: "If you tell someone I will do something worse to myself" or "You are the only one that knows" or "You are the only one I trust". It is really rare that those things are true. That takes a while for young people to realise that.'

No School is Perfect

Young people do not benefit from parents and schools being in conflict. It is in their best interests to work together and ensure young people are still progressively made responsible for their behaviour both at home and school. Many issues seen at home do surface at school but may surface in different ways and may also be managed very differently due to the context.

Parents who go to the school for help should be met with caring and appropriate support. However, parents do need to recognise the reality of the school context and the limitations that teachers have while dealing with classrooms full of children. Errors in judgement, misunderstandings and time pressures all affect communication. Schools that deliberately build a culture of care and positivity deal with self-harm in a much more compassionate way.

Concluding Thoughts

External support can provide perspective, hope and skills to move any challenging time forward. Educating teachers and continuing to lift the shame associated with self-harm will make it easier for young people and their families to access support. The next chapter is super practical. It is filled with practical strategies to beat self-harm by replacing with it with self-care. We will also talk about harm minimisation and safety plans, which are an essential part of recovery for some young people.

Key Insights from this Chapter

- It is very common for young people to feel awkward or ashamed when their parents find out about self-harm.
- A third party such as a psychologist, counsellor or mentor

might be a good neutral person for a young person to talk to.
- For many, getting young people to talk to a professional can be as difficult as 'selling ice to an Eskimo'. Evidence suggests that most young people are reluctant to access professional support for mental health problems.
- I want to emphasise that a professional can't replace parents. You can't hand parenting over to anyone else. Please show up, in real life and counselling sessions, every time, whole heartedly.
- We need to listen to what is working or not working for them and why. Trust, rapport and a positive experience are huge factors in engaging any young person in therapeutic relationships.
- Each school has an internal referral system, which usually progresses from teaching staff through to school counsellors, then to parents and external referrals. While no system is perfect, I have found that every school has within it

champions of young people's mental health.
- Teachers, like parents, find self-harm confronting and may not always be educated in how to approach it or what to do.
- Self-harm is an intensely private issue, which often needs to be dealt with in such a way that respects this.

7

Self-Care and Safety Plans

Typically, treatment of self-harm can be challenging. That is why we need to keep our minds open to a variety of intervention methods available to young people. One size does not fit all. I have found that clinical methods have limited success for many young people, and therefore more holistic approaches have needed to be sought out by families. Parents, be as creative as you need to be. Do what works.

This is my simple but helpful formula, which I have used time and time again with young people who are in the very early phases of self-harm. This, coupled with a safety plan (which you will find later in this Chapter) is a great starting place for a young person who is ready to beat self-harm.

As you view these stages, realise that young people may jump between them as they progress. Stages can overlap. Sometimes it may seem like they make progress, only to start back at Stage 1 again. This is all very normal.

Stage 1: Professional and Parental Support

When young people come to my office for support, their life usually looks like this. They are flapping in the air, out of control, with the negatives dominating their life. They usually need the help of a caring adult to lift some of the 'heaviest boxes' out of the way. You will always see the 'big four' when you read about poor mental health: medication, therapy, exercise and sleep.

These are usually the 'big boxes' that need moving.

Medication might come in the form of prescription drugs, diet changes or natural remedies. Therapy might include talking to a psychologist, mentor or dedicated family member. Exercise might be as simple as enrolling in a team sport or using a personal trainer. Sleep is a difficult one to control but is usually a by-product of establishing healthy and happy day-to-day routine. Apps like 'Sleep Cycle' can be used to monitor sleep patterns. Be as creative as necessary in order to move these 'big boxes' out of the way. Be careful to listen to the young person so you hear what is actually working or not working for them.

Stage 2: Self-Care

One of the questions parents ask me the most is, 'When do I step in and when do I let go?'

It can be understandably hard for parents to let go of a child who has been struggling, as they don't want them to encounter any further pain. Once a young person is balancing in the 'middle' position, they are reasonably stable. They are out of the danger zone. Things could go up or down at any stage, but they are in a position where they are clear headed enough to make decisions and learn from mistakes.

This is the point where parents need to let go of caring for a young person's basic needs, as the young person needs to discover which self-care strategies work for them. These are critical skills that they can't learn if they are over-parented. Therapeutic relationships that help young people develop self-awareness, talk through heavy emotions and implement self-care strategies are usually a critical part of this phase.

Sometimes young people are resistant to caring for themselves and would prefer that others meet their needs. They may be comfortable having parents or family members do this. Parents may feel forced to 'pamper' to them and may feel controlled by manipulative behaviour. It is important that parents identify this behaviour as unhealthy.

Parents should also realise that self-care doesn't mean young people are free to parent themselves. Parents shouldn't negate parenting responsibilities in an attempt to 'let go'; their children still need the same boundaries they have always needed.

Stage 3: Self-Mastery

This is what life looks like when a young person's resources for coping are stronger than their pain. Of course, they don't stay grounded all of the time. Wouldn't that be nice?! However, they have found self-care strategies that work for them and they have the maturity to implement them consistently. We can't expect young people to find this self-mastery overnight. The reality is that this position takes time and practice to master.

Delay. Distract. Decide.

The opposite of self-harm is self-care. Ideally, we want young people to practise self-care to regulate their emotions and avoid the overwhelming spiral that leads to self-harm. Simple in theory; not so simple in practice.

As a foundation for self-care, young people need to develop an awareness of how they feel, and recognise when they need to begin to implement self-care strategies. Identifying emotions can be difficult for some young people, especially if they have experienced trauma. In these cases, a psychologist may be the best person to help them identify and express appropriate emotions.

Emotions demand movement. When emotions are escalating, they quickly move young people in either a positive or negative direction. The good news is that young people can choose which direction they will follow. Self-care will always move a young person in a positive direction. Even a negative situation has the capacity to move a young person positively if they understand how to care for themselves. The more educated young people are, the more self-care options they have to choose from.

Emotions, just like waves, have a limited life span. When a young person practices self-care they ride the wave of intense emotion until it passes. It is important to remember that all emotions we experience, whether happy or sad, have a limited life span. Self-care is a courageous decision to make, because it takes effort and strength.

The basic premise for riding an emotional wave can be seen in

Cognitive Behaviour Therapist Carol Vivyan's *3D's: Delay, Distract, Decide* journal activity, which I saw on the wall of a school classroom many years ago.

Delay: Delay giving in to the urge of self-harm for a set amount of time. *You* get to decide on how long that time will be. You can set a timer if you want to ensure you stick to the time you decide on.

Distract: Do an activity that can occupy your thoughts and channel your energy in a positive direction. Write a list of things you could do. This list can be written in advance.

Decide: After the set period, decide how you are going to respond to the urge. Write down the advantages and disadvantages of delaying the urge again, if it is still there.

It is interesting to consider the time frames between thoughts and actions, and how self-care may play a part in helping young people avoid self-harm in these time frames:

- 40% of young people decided to self-harm within one hour

- 22.7% of young people decided to self-harm in more than an hour but less than a week
- 29.3% of young people who decided to self-harm made the decision more than one week before

Young people may consider a wider range of self-care strategies that may help them ride a wave of intense emotions. Each individual will have a preference or type of self-care that works best for them, based on why they self-harm and the typical length of time between their thoughts about self-harming and corresponding actions.

Creative self-care strategies:

- Story writing
- Painting, drawing and other art forms
- Journaling
- Composing music or playing instruments
- Compiling music playlists
- Putting on makeup or styling hair
- Learning a new skill or art form

Soothing self-care strategies:

- Taking a warm bath or shower
- Putting on comfortable clothes
- Buying different textured socks
- Drinking hot milk
- Cuddling a teddy bear or blanket
- Getting a massage
- Putting on perfume or lighting a scented candle
- Watching TV or a movie

Organising self-care strategies:

- Sorting a wardrobe
- Cleaning a bedroom
- Building something
- Reorganising makeup
- Finishing homework or assignments

Social self-care strategies:

- Phoning a friend
- Being with a friend
- Helping someone else in need
- Going to a public place
- Gaming with friends

- Watching funny YouTube videos with friends
- Playing with a pet

Physical self-care strategies:

- Riding a bike or going for a run
- Dancing
- Squeezing something
- Making a loud noise
- Ripping something
- Punching something
- Eating something with a strong taste

Meditation is arguably a lost art in our society. Some people use relaxation music to purposefully empty their minds. Yoga and mindfulness are all tools that young people can use to focus their energy. Sitting and doing nothing will work well too. Young people often need some quiet time alone, just to let their mind relax and refresh.

Apps that I recommend and work with:
- #selfcare
- Calm Harm
- Mood Path

- The Breathing APP
- Sleep Cycle
- Smiling Mind

The 'Calm Harm' app guides young people through a similar process to the 3D Journal Activity.

Strategies I Have Seen Work

One strategy I have seen work is asking young people to draw the name of someone they love in the place that they usually self-harm. Alternatively, they could put a fake tattoo or an inspiring quote in that place. This may act as a reminder as to why they are choosing not to self-harm.

Another strategy that I have seen work is replacing self-harm with body painting. I encourage parents to buy soft paintbrushes of varying sizes and colourful paints so young people can paint their arms, legs or other parts of their body that they would usually harm. Young people tell me that the 'sensory experience is soothing, and the strokes of colour bring hope'. One young lady explains, 'I have been photographing and documenting my body art. It gives me something to look back on with pride and joy. I can share my art with my family and it sometimes helps me open up and talk about my struggles.' One chaplain contacted me and explained, 'I now have a few pots of body paint in my chappy room, and some coloured eyeliner pencils for "henna tattoo" art that young people can use if they are feeling overwhelmed. It's a great alternative to self-harming.'

Teaching Self Care

Knowing how to manage emotions and comfort yourself when you are unhappy or distressed is a skill that can take anyone a long time to learn. Even grown adults look for someone else to comfort and rescue them! Why? Because it takes self-perception to find strategies that truly work, because we are always growing and evolving as human beings.

How we self-care changes according to the stage of life that we are in. Self-care for a two-year-old is very different to self-care for a 12-year-old and a 30-year-old. Renegotiating what your self-care looks like in each stage of your life requires a reassessment of what is working and what is not working. Self-care requires you look at your entire life to discover what you need next. It takes foresight.

Because young people are prone to looking externally instead of looking internally, they often copy the self-care strategies of others. They may look at what the reality TV stars do or what their friends do. I find that young people's down time is often spent wishing they were someone else or somewhere else, instead of truly nurturing themselves and being honest about who they are and what fills them with joy.

We can get stuck seeing our teenagers like children and not allowing them the opportunity to explore self-care strategies for themselves. I find that mums try to manage this area of their young people's lives. I hear mums say, 'If they are going to act like a child I am going to treat them like a child.' Unfortunately, what worked for them as a child won't work for them as a teenager, regardless of their childish behaviour. We might offer them the self-care strategies that used to work for them when they were younger, such as staying home to rest or going out as a family. Yet dictated methods of self-care seldom work. Self-care strategies work because they bring reward or perceived reward.

During puberty our young people have to experiment and find new ways of coping. As parents we have to be flexible in allowing this process to happen. Sometimes we are too rigid and hold on to what worked for us when our kids were young. We can be working with the old game book even when young people have written several updated editions. Cut them some slack. Long periods of time in their bedroom can be a normal part of self-discovery, as may be a frequent desire to socialise.

I see great value in our young people participating in self-care strategies that they may not currently use. Families may deliberately work self-care into their family's daily routine for everyone's benefit. For example: setting aside time to talk, cooking healthy food together or exercising together. Adding self-care strategies into a family routine enables young people to broaden their self-care skills and adopt strategies that may be different from their own.

Harm Minimisation

If you have a young person who self-harms regularly, you will know that breaking the habit can be very challenging. Self-care strategies may sound like an overly simplistic, incomplete solution to a very complex issue. During these times, a harm-minimisation approach may be suggested by a therapist.

Harm minimisation has its strongest history in the field of substance misuse. When applied to self-harm, harm minimisation acknowledges that self-harm is likely to occur and accepts that a young person may choose to use it at a given point in their life. The focus is on supporting a young person, rather than ceasing the self-harm. It is an alternative to a zero-tolerance approach.

Professionals may explore less destructive or harmful methods of self-harm and suggest that young people only do what is essential for emotional relief. This ensures young people do the least amount of damage to themselves and others.

It can be very confronting – even overwhelming – for parents to accept they can't control a young person's desire to self-harm, and therefore minimisation strategies are often best discussed in consultation with professionals. The more intensely and frequently a young person self-harms, the more likely a harm-minimisation approach will be needed. Young people are much more likely to harm themselves badly if they have used a dangerous or violent method, use self-harm regularly and have an increased tolerance of pain, are physically isolated or have a mental illness.

This approach is understandably often a last resort for parents who would prefer their young person to simply *stop* self-harming. It may also be a temporary approach until they are ready to adopt healthier coping strategies.

Self-harm alternatives such as flicking a rubber band on one's wrist, eating a hot chilli, having a freezing cold shower, drawing red lines where a young person usually cuts or holding ice on the body until it burns, are commonly suggested harm-minimisation strategies. The colour red is often used in harm-minimisation strategies, either in red-dyed ice cubes or red coloured pens. This is because the sight of red to mimic blood is an important part of the self-harm process.

These strategies obviously cause less harm than cutting or burning, but I have never seen them satisfy a young person's determined urge to self-harm. Young people have to be prepared to give themselves some 'harmless pain' to voluntarily use these strategies. In the same way that young people have to *choose* to self-care they also have to choose to adopt a harm-minimisation approach.

Making sure wounds are cared for properly is also an important part of harm minimisation. Young people can reduce the risk of infection by using clean blades and dressings. If parents are ever worried about a wound or injury they should contact emergency or their local hospital.

I had the privilege of mentoring Eunice for many years, and worked with her in conjunction with psychologists, psychiatrists and general practitioners. You can find her full story in Chapter 10. It took Eunice quite a number of years to develop healthier coping strategies and fully embrace self-care. This quote, from Eunice's mum, gives some insights into why a harm-minimisation approach was chosen during the latter stages of Eunice's recovery:

> Michelle has been helping my daughter handle disappointment. She tends to blame me and her teachers if things don't go to plan or her way. She has to learn that sometimes life doesn't go to plan, and no one can be blamed. She is slowly starting to take ownership of her feelings and reactions. She used to cut every day and now she is only cutting once a week on

average and has even gone a period of three weeks without cutting. I used to take all the blades in the house away and somehow, she managed to find other ones. I used to check through all the draws for sharpeners, scissors and knives. After about a year of doing that I gave up looking for blades. I told her if she wants to change she will have to take responsibility for changing. I can't do it for her. I had to accept where she was at.

Ready to Stop?

There is a big difference between young people saying they want to stop self-harm and actually being ready to stop self-harm. These questions below will give parents and their children an indication of whether the young people are really ready to make the commitment to stop self-harming. They are an important first step for young people to be able to answer.

- Do I believe I really want to stop hurting myself? Is it my idea or someone else's?
- Why do I want to stop hurting myself? Do I have a substantial reason?
- Are there at least two people who are willing to help me stop?
- Do I know what usually triggers my self-harm?
- Do I know how I feel before I self-harm?
- Am I willing to tolerate negative feelings? When is a time when I have done this?
- Do I have a professional that I can turn to for support?

The Importance of Safety Plans

I spoke to Demi, who shared her experiences with a male friend whose self-harm resulted in suicide. She told me:

> I had a friend who committed suicide last year. Travis was a close friend at school and everyone knew him. It affected a lot of people. We

found out that his ten-year-old brother found him hanging in a tree. The school teachers went to the funeral. We all went to the funeral. His mum was pretty upset, and it affected us all so much. It affected me so much that I don't want to self-harm. I think he used to take all his self-harm out on drugs. I know he used to take drugs to self-harm. He used drugs and he didn't take care of himself. I think he self-harmed a long time before he hung himself.

The very sad reality is that we must discuss safety with young people, even if they are hard discussions to have. Safety plans are realistic, 'how-to' plans, and are particularly important if there is any risk of significant injury or suicide. This is a template that I have used with families. I have asked a 15-year-old girl to fill it in, so you can see it in use.

Self-Harm Safety Plan

Melissa's Safety Plan

Warning Signs (behaviour changes, mood changes) that indicate things are escalating:
- A mood change – anxious or mad
- I don't want to be around people and in my room more
- Starting to get snappy (erupt at someone like my brother)

Self-Care Strategies (I can do alone)
- A face mask
- Play music (makes me happier) ps. Stay off my phone that doesn't help much.
- My dog makes me happy

Self-Care Strategies (I can do with people)
- Facetime my GOOD friend about normal stuff or even organising go out with a friend
- Go out with a friend if I can
- Being around the family in general and not be alone

People I Can Contact
- My mum
- My older sister
- My cousin

Their Recommended Self-Care Strategies
- Go for a walk or run (get out of the house)
- Stay with the family even if I don't want to
- Watch a movie

Professional Agencies I can contact
- My psychologist
- My doctor if I had to
- I guess I could call a helpline

Harm Minimisation Strategies
- If I had to harm in front of mum I wouldn't hurt myself that much. That is actually what we have talked about. That is what she would rather me do.
- Not to cut deep
- To take care of the cuts

One Reason Why Life is Worth Living
- I have a family who I can rely on and I have friends

The Last Time I Self-Harmed

I am always intrigued to find out why young people stopped self-harming. That is why I try to ask those who have given up the habit about their last experience. So many of them tell me that 'it didn't give them the relief the expected' or they 'woke up to themselves'. Here are three stories from young ladies who share about the last time they self-harmed with me.

Amanda's Story

Amanda self-harmed for many years and built up quite a tolerance for the pain associated with it. When she was 19, she and her boyfriend had a huge fight, which led to them breaking up. She was devastated. Self-harm was her usual coping strategy, so she took a blade to her stomach and, in her words, 'cut it to pieces'. Amanda thought the pain would be tolerable, but when she woke up the next morning it was like nothing she had ever experienced. She was in agony. Surprisingly she never presented to hospital and the wounds eventually healed. At that moment Amanda promised herself that she would never cut again – and she didn't. That was enough to negatively associate self-harm with pain instead of relief.

Milly's Story

I am not even sure I can recall the last time I self-harmed. It was over a year ago now. My mum might know better than me! I just started to feel like I had grown out of it and I didn't need to do it anymore. The thought of it slowly started to drop off.

Melissa's Story

Something happened. I can't remember what I was, that is how insignificant it was. I went into the shower and I got my scissors and I started cutting. My sister came in to get something out of the shower and she yelled out to Mum, 'Melissa is cutting again.' Mum came running in and it was really messy. Everyone was yelling. I have no idea why that was the last time I cut. I hadn't done it for ages.

Concluding Thoughts

A parent's greatest challenge is to listen to a young person and accept their current state of mind. When a parent does this they guide rather than take control of the process. Being realistic about young people's intention will help professionals and parents determine which strategies are best suited to support them. In the next chapter we are going to talk about positivity, hope, gratitude and belonging – all important things to underpin a young person's mental health.

Key Insights from this Chapter

- Typically, treatment of self-harm can be challenging. That is why we need to keep our minds open to a variety of intervention methods

available to young people. One size does not fit all.
- You will always see the 'big four' when you read about poor mental health: medication, therapy, exercise and sleep. These are usually the 'big boxes' that young people need help moving.
- The opposite of self-harm is self-care. Ideally, we want young people to practise self-care to regulate their emotions and avoid the overwhelming spiral that leads to self-harm.
- Self-care is simple in theory; not so simple in practice.
- Emotions demand movement. When emotions are escalating, they quickly move young people in either a positive or negative direction. The good news is that young people can choose which direction they will follow. Self-care will always move a young person in a positive direction.
- Emotions, just like waves, have a limited life span. When a young person practices self-care they ride

the wave of intense emotion until it passes.
- Each individual will have a preference or type of self-care that works best for them, based on why they self-harm and the typical length of time between their thoughts about self-harming and corresponding actions.
- Harm minimisation acknowledges that self-harm is likely to occur and accepts that a young person may choose to use it at a given point in their life. The focus is on supporting a young person, rather than ceasing the self-harm. It is an alternative to a zero-tolerance approach.
- Safety plans are realistic, 'how-to' plans, and are particularly important if there is any risk of significant injury or suicide.
- Self-care is a courageous decision to make, because it takes effort and strength.

8

Parent as Coach

The Child & Adolescent Self-harm in Europe (CASE) Study (2008) conducted a school-based survey of 30,000 adolescents. It found:
- 79.6% had not experienced thoughts of self-harm
- 14.6% had thoughts about self-harm but had not taken action
- 2.6% reported a single incident
- 3.2% reported multiple episodes

The above statistics show that 14.6% of young people had thoughts about self-harm that they had not acted upon. This indicates a real need for preventative services that address destructive thinking before the actual behaviour starts. When I work with young people I listen for 'self-harm thinking', not just self-harm behaviour. I respond to the thinking, whether the harm is evident or not.

As we have previously discussed, there are some precursors to self-harm that we need to take into account. Poor mental health (anxiety, depression, impulsivity and risk taking), plus stressful life events (including family issues or personal pain) make young people more susceptible to self-harm. Increased frequency and severity of self-harm are associated with an increased combination of these elements. Young people displaying any of these need all the preventative strategies we can provide.

Transition times are the times when we need to keep our hearts tuned to the pressure around our young ones and older ones alike. The last year of school is a big transition time for our kids, as is the entrance into high school. Rachael Rubio, has been good enough to share her personal journey with us in Chapter 10 of this book. She also shares wisdom, saying, 'Confident kids are unlikely to use self-harm as a method for coping. All kids are likely to go through times when their self-esteem isn't strong. As parents we need to be looking out for those times. We need to particularly watch out for transitional times – primary to high school, changing schools, change in friendship groups, going through puberty...'

I recently had a young girl who was in Year 7 approach me after a presentation I delivered in a local school about stress and anxiety. She wanted my help as she had a piano exam in the days following. She was very worried about the exam. I asked her what her biggest concerns were, and she said, 'I don't know how I am going to cope if I don't do well.' My heart heard her. It is imperative to handle these key times in their lives with care and a watchful eye. We don't always see self-harm – we hear it.

That Word: Resilience

In my book *Everyday Resilience: Helping Kids Handle Friendship Drama, Academic Pressure and the Self-Doubt of Growing Up,* I talk about how to storm-proof children, and build resilience by using the micro moments of everyday life. This book is a great resource for parents whose children are self-harming, as resilience is exactly what our children need to make it through life's challenges.

Resilience is the ability to adapt in the face of adversity, trauma, tragedy, threats, stress, strained family relationships or problems. The ability to recover from setbacks in order to keep going in the face of adversity is something that we need to foster in young people. They certainly will need it throughout life.

People have trouble making the connection between self-harm and resilience. They find it easier to connect self-harm to self-care. Think of self-care like the immediate substitute for self-harm, and resilience strategies the strong foundation to build on.

The best way I can help parents understand the role they play in developing resilience is by using the following analogy.

Think about a young person's life like a big gym session (with lots of squats), and a parent's role like a personal trainer. Young people need our help to develop a tolerance for 'the burn' that comes from doing life's squats. We must help them develop capacity for emotional pain that inevitably happens in life as they live, grow, fail, get up again, fail some more and conquer their dreams. They should know how to respond when they meet resistance.

We don't want our young people to push past their emotional capacity to the point of burnout, but we do want them to know how to work with the burn and get another five squats out of themselves without breaking down. This requires a mental strength that says, 'I can handle this.'

Our job as parent coach is critical. A poor coach would allow them to sit the session out every time the burn starts. He or she would pull up a chair for the young person, bring them a Coke and say, 'Take a rest. Sit this one out. I know we are supposed to be training today but you look tired. There is always tomorrow.'

A great coach will probably do the opposite. He or she might say, 'You can do it. You've only got five more squats to go. Stay focused. Let me wipe your sweat. Let me count you down. If you need to shake it out, that's okay. If you need to breathe, breathe. Your goals are worth it.'

A great coach finds 101 ways to say, 'I believe you can'.

There is a real art to saying, 'I believe you can' creatively. Remind them of their strengths, abilities, relationships, innate worth as a human being and physical attributes. In my book *Parenting Teenage Girls in the Age of a New Normal* I talk about 'hitting and running' praise because teenagers often reject their parents' compliments, especially if they are struggling with a negative state of mind.

This is how 'hit and run' praise works. Get within earshot of them, compliment them and then disappear. You might like to say, 'That new colour looks great in your hair', or 'Nice job with the dishes', or even, 'I'm really proud of you'. The trick is, don't stick around to see them roll their eyes or give you a cheeky reply. Get out of there in a hurry. Don't make it a big deal.

Teenagers still need to hear how much you love them and what you love about them, even though they deny it.

I try to 'hit and run' my kids a few times a day. It balances out all the negatives I address as a parent. As I walk away I imagine their reaction and I sometimes even roll my eyes for them.

Young people lean heavily on stable adults for perspective and hope. I had coffee with a mum today who shared her teenage journey with me. She ran into a series of disappointments at the end of school, which she admittedly didn't handle well. She lost her optimism and way. Unfortunately, she didn't have a caring adult in her life to guide her.

'What happens if you don't have anyone in your life that is telling you there is a plan beyond what you are currently feeling ... someone encouraging you when the tough times come...?' she asked. 'I didn't know what I didn't know.'

'I guess you just make up the ending according to the limited knowledge you have,' I responded. 'When you are a teenager the one thing you lack is perspective. You think life is always going to feel like it does "today". I find that young people lean heavily on me for perspective and hope. That's my role in their lives.'

The Power of Gratitude

Optimism is a shield that does come more naturally to some than others. Some young people have a genetically lower happiness set point than others, and there are specific things we can do to help them along the way. Robert Emmons has written some excellent content in this area in his book *Thanks!*. His research shows a solid connection between gratitude and the health of a person psychologically, physically and socially. I therefore conclude that it is a really important skill to develop in young people who are struggling with self-harm or any destructive behaviour.

Annette Spur, who has been a spokesperson for Australia's National Day of Thanks for nearly ten years, shared with me her thoughts about gratitude and the impact it has had on her life and health. Annette struggled with post-natal depression and recognised that gratitude was going to be a key factor in her recovery. It took practice for her to find things to be grateful for each night as she journaled. One quote that really inspired her was:

If you woke up today with only the things you were grateful for yesterday, what would you wake up with?

In her experience practice made perfect. But with practice, every negative situation was able to be turned into a positive. She said, 'When something goes wrong I focus on the positives and I feel a sense of wellbeing.' This type of mindset that is able to flip a negative into a positive is not something that comes naturally to young people.

Annette also commented, 'We aren't born grateful. We are born entitled. You ask any baby who misses their 5a.m. feed and you won't find them grateful. When things don't go our way in life, gratitude is not our natural reaction. Gratitude is learned. It is up to parents to teach it.'

My mother placed a lot of value on being grateful for what we had and what we were given. When someone gave me a gift it felt like the whole world stopped and she stared until I said the magic words, 'thank you'. However, fast forward my life 13 years and the best word to describe me was ungrateful. My parents had brought me up well, but I had grown as most teenagers grow: entitled.

If this sounds like your child, be assured that you are not alone or unusual. In fact, young people are developmentally egocentric. Coaching gratefulness in young people – especially young people who may be struggling with poor mental health or challenging life circumstances – is no easy task. It can be very difficult to open up their minds to the world beyond themselves.

I have noticed that we are reluctant to talk about gratitude with young people who are going through a hard time because we don't want to offend them in their current mindset. However, I believe our reluctance does them a great disservice.

There is power in gratitude. There is also power in loving and in challenging an unhealthy mindset.

Tegan's Story

About a year ago I was approached by a mother of three. Her youngest daughter had a disability. Tegan, her eldest, had hit puberty and built up some resentment about the amount of time her mother was spending with her younger sister. Any family who has a child with a disability knows how tough it can be. This had to be acknowledged.

Tegan was surrounded by girlfriends who were cutting. She had very, very tiny scratches on her thighs. She was, understandably, crying for attention. Her mother was horribly scared that self-harm was going to take hold of her daughter and was responding with all guns blazing. She was the best mother a girl could have.

We met and talked. Mum cried. I thought about offering suggestions like 'Take your daughter out by herself once a week', 'Buy her a bracelet to remind her how loved she is', or 'Write her a meaningful letter'. And all those things could have been said, but my guess was that her mother was already doing all those things and there was still a gaping hole. Usually mums end up talking to me once they have tried the obvious!

I know that you parents out there reading this book have tried all the obvious things. I get it. All the commonsense things just aren't working – or at least not quickly. My guess is that you are reading this book because it's not simple, and 2+2 isn't adding up to 4.

I remember sending a mum out of the room and sitting alone with her dear girl. I prepared her for a tough conversation by saying this: 'I want you to promise me that at the end of this conversation you and I are still going to be friends.' That was the best way I knew how to say, 'Things are about to get awkward.' She was ready to talk about cutting, so it made it easy for me to have a direct conversation.

For the next 45 minutes I told her that I couldn't, in good conscience, tell her that she had a life that was worth cutting away. I reminded her that the mum who was in the waiting room loved her more than life itself, that she had a roof over her head, food on the table and a school that would bend over backwards to support her. Small things in a privileged society, but worth noting.

I promised her that the way forward would not be found by focusing on her disappointment, regardless of how deep those disappointments were. Then we had a marshmallow break! We were still friends. In fact, she was smiling. It's amazing what a bit of truth said in love can do to inspire someone's heart.

We also spoke about the benefits that her disappointments could bring to her life. Disappointments were like gold. To find the gold we would have to wade into the darkest of areas, find a shovel and deliberately dig. I truly believe that if young people can take their toughest moment and find gratitude in THAT moment, that will be their secret for success for the rest of their lives. If I could help Tegan find her gold I would be incredibly satisfied! That would be her story. That would be her strength for the rest of her life.

Parents, I know we want to hand our child perfection – but we can't. Whether it be a divorce, bankruptcy or health issues, we all end up offering our children a disappointment in one form or another. It's impossible to sidestep all of life's challenges. However, I believe that it is that very divorce, bankruptcy, or other hardship that could be the secret to your child's happiness for the rest of their lives. It's not the absence of hardship, but the lessons that come from the hardship itself that will make a young person a strong human being. Gratitude for the hardest times will be your young person's recipe for success for the rest of their life.

I believe that real life has to be enough for our kids to find happiness in. I have had to believe that each young person's reality is enough. If I didn't believe that, I would have given up hope a long time ago. I have seen young people and families go through some extremely tough things and come out the other side with a strong sense of hope and determination for their future. It *is* possible.

I gave Tegan a gratitude journal that helped her identify things she could be thankful for every day – things that may already be passing through her mind that she wasn't fully recognising. We had to train her brain to find positives in the simple things. It really does take practice. Sometimes she felt like the journal was annoying and silly. Sometimes she saw value in it.

We met every week, and that's when we really started digging for gold. I helped her pick up her shovel. Piece by piece, gem by gem, we found treasure. I wanted to help her find what made her life special, unique and valuable to the world. Why did she want to be a part of *her* family and no one else's?

Some weeks we made progress and other weeks it felt like we didn't. The most beautiful revelation that young lady had was that she didn't want to be anyone else's daughter but her mum's. Why? Tegan decided that her mum was the only mum who could teach her courage, strength and love. She was grateful for her mum, and to belong to her mum. That right there made a huge difference. That was her turning point. Self-care is essential. Gratitude requires maturity, but it works for the long haul.

In his talk *Thanks! The Benefits of Gratitude* Emmon talks about gratitude as its impact on social relationships, because gratitude is a social emotion. It has been referred to as a social strengthening emotion. It involves perception of being supported and affirmed by other people, which changes the benefit and the nature of the relationship now between the individuals. Through gratitude they themselves can become more helpful, outgoing, pro-social, generous, compassionate, less isolated, less lonely, more positive and less destructive.

Emmon's research describes how I saw gratitude work in Tegan's life. It transformed how she viewed her mother and interacted with her family, making her more aware of the positives and also her ability to contribute to the home. In a generation who have been called entitled, we must cultivate gratitude as a defence against the destructive thinking that wants to rob young people of seeing the love they are surrounded with.

Ways to Be Thankful

I am not suggesting that you try this exact 'pick up your shovel' conversation with your son or daughter. The parent/child relationship has its limits! What I would suggest is that there are ways you can incorporate gratitude into your everyday conversations that will remind you that you have each other, and that is easy to forget. When things get tough it is easy to focus on pain rather than the things around us that are available to bring us joy.

Our language regarding failure, pain and stress is something we should be very conscious of. Failure is something we can choose to embrace and celebrate in our homes as a learning opportunity. Pain is an important motivator for learning. It's in the embracing of pain and failure that we truly thrive as human beings. If we can teach our children to embrace failure, we are doing a remarkable job as parents.

Daily conversations starters like, 'Tell me two things that went well today', 'Talk to me about two people who you admire', 'Talk to me about three beautiful things in your life', 'Tell me three reasons why I love you' or 'Let's talk about something that we are looking forward to' train a young person's brain to see a glass half full rather than half empty.

Remember: find ways to tell them that they *can,* ways to see things from a positive perspective and ways to be grateful.

And when they are ready to formally dig into gratitude, here are some resources that I recommend:
- The Resilience Project APP
- The 30-Day Gratitude Challenge

The Power of Belonging

Ideally a sense of belonging is something that should underpin every child's life. Research suggests that young people who are brought up with a strong sense of belonging have less risk of engaging in other harmful behaviours. Belonging is a strong protection against mental health and a powerful motivator to keeping them on track. People who belong have a better sense of motivation and happiness.

Many families face non-ideal situations where divorce, separation due to conflict, cultural or financial commitments, or death challenge a young person's sense of family belonging. In these situations, families have to work harder to keep a sense of security around young people who may feel abandoned, rejected or neglected. Single parents distinctly know the challenge of bringing up children on their own. So do families who have moved countries and are not surrounded by extended family.

Breaking down the meaning and value of belonging gives us a better idea of its importance. It also helps us realise that it isn't about a specific family unit. Whatever your family is, belonging is attainable and there are specific things we can do to help build a sense of belonging in our homes.

Belonging means to be accepted as part of a member of a team. Belonging is a human need just like a need for food, and it is essential when it comes to processing intense emotions. Belonging to a family who love us unconditionally is invaluable. People seek out community, social or sporting groups to further meet their emotional need to belong.

Belonging to a group validates who you are. When a group accepts you, they are validating you. Validation is the acknowledgement that someone believes in your worth. Validation is powerful. In the same way we need to find ways to tell young people they *can,* we also need to find ways to tell people they *belong.*

Telling young people that they are an important and loved part of the family – that the family wouldn't be the same without them and they are legitimately needed – is a way that we can build a sense of belonging around their lives.

Belonging is also about giving young people a sense of ownership and understanding of who they are in their world. They need to feel legitimately needed. That is why chores are not just chores – they are about young people owning their place in the home. It is easy to do everything ourselves, but it doesn't reinforce belonging. Creating environments where their contribution matters and is relied on is critical for their sense of belonging. What do they do around the house that others can't live without? How are they needed?

Routine and rituals that reinforce togetherness and that young people look forward to are under-rated in our culture. These routines knit families together and provide a sense of belonging that can't be found anywhere else in their lives. Monday night 'family nights'. 'Thursday night football', 'Lazy Saturday breakfasts' or Sunday nights together. These *could* include doing chores and cooking meals together.

When is the next time your family is looking forward to getting together?

Concluding Thoughts

When it comes to beating self-harm, we can't underestimate the benefit that positivity, gratitude, hope and belonging provide. The more creatively and subtly we can incorporate these things into our lives, the more we can support young people's mental health. Keeping the dynamics of the home safe and happy is so important, that is why I have dedicated the next chapter to 'Taking Care of Family".

Key Insights from this Chapter

- When we need to keep our hearts tuned to the pressure around young people during transition times.
- Resilience is the ability to adapt in the face of adversity, trauma, tragedy, threats, stress, strained family relationships or problems. The ability to recover from setbacks in order to keep going in the face

of adversity is something that we need to foster in young people.
- We should parent every day with resilience in mind.
- Parents may like to think about a young person's life like a big gym session (with lots of squats), and a parent's role like a personal trainer.
- Young people need our help to develop a tolerance for 'the burn' that comes from doing life's squats. We must help them develop capacity for emotional pain that inevitably happens in life as they live, grow, fail, get up again, fail some more and conquer their dreams. They should know how to respond when they meet resistance.
- We don't want our young people to push past their emotional capacity to the point of burnout, but we do want them to know how to work with the burn and get another five squats out of themselves without breaking down. This requires a mental strength that says, 'I can handle this.'
- Optimism is a shield that does come more naturally to some than others.

- There is power in gratitude. There is also power in loving and in challenging an unhealthy mindset.

9
Taking Care of Family

Once initial reactions have passed, the full weight of self-harm begins to take its toll on families. Parents talk to me about sleepless nights and high anxiety in the weeks and sometimes months to follow. Sometimes parents recall sleeping in or near their young person's room out of fear they will harm themselves. Other times, parents tell me they stay up through the night researching support services on the internet. All of this takes its toll on parenting styles and strategies, siblings, marriages, and even finances.

According to *The Impact of Self-harm by Young People on Parents and Families*, parents' secondary reactions to self-harm include stress, anxiety, guilt and, in some cases, clinical depression. 'I ended up seeing a psychologist and going on anti-depressants myself. It just exhausted me to the point that I wasn't sleeping. I was constantly worried about her hurting herself,' said Debra, mother of three.

On top of this, parents are coping with the very real stigma associated with self-harm. In an overwhelming desire to keep issues private and avoid being judged by others who may not understand, parents often withdraw from friends and family. This may include saying no to holiday invitations, trips to the beach and nights out. It becomes challenging to look after yourself and family when your innate instinct is to isolate yourself from your usually support networks.

This is a story written by a mother, which describes her very full-on experience with her son who self-harmed. It is as raw and as real a tale as any mother who experiences significant self-harm can tell. As you read it I want you to notice the emotional journey this mother would have been on. The undeniable urge to protect your own flesh and blood is palpable. There is a place of necessary intervention which in many cases only a parent is available to provide. There is also a place of letting go when the time allows, which is just as essential for a parent's self-care as a young person's sense of self.

Our eldest son cut deep. He cut to bleed. The bleeding was important to him, it was to let the pain out. He also attempted to hang himself by tying his school neck tie around his throat and knotting the other end to the ceiling fan. He didn't want to die, he wanted to hurt himself, the physical actions giving a sense of meaning to the pain he felt deep inside.

He was in Year 7. He wore big baggy jumpers and it was really obvious what was going on. It would be in the middle of summer in Queensland and he would be the only kid with long sleeves on.

We thought if we put away sharp instruments we'd protect him, but it seemed to be an overwhelming urge that needed to be satisfied ... even if it meant using a broken pencil to achieve that. At times I had to try and physically restrain him, especially when I feared where the emotions would take him. I even wrestled him fully clothed into a shower on two occasions.

During those really bad times there was no talking sense into him ... other times where I could catch him before he fell too far into the blackness. I'd either bundle him in the car and drive or I'd make him walk the block with me. The act of doing something side by side, without the fear of seeing what's in your eyes is often the best place for the deepest conversations.

Often times my husband was at work and there were times when I would have to get my daughter to call him to come home to help me. It was overwhelming.

We were referred to a paediatrician by a GP. A few paediatricians later, he was diagnosed with Asperger's and put on Risperdal which is an antipsychotic. Things started to make sense and come good. The onset of puberty really impacted him. We don't have a history of mental health in my family but my brother has ADHD so this was all new to us.

There were times where I would call the doctors and they would tell me to admit him to hospital, but I couldn't do that to a 12-year-old. That's the reality of living through this with a child with mental health issues. There are limited options when they are adolescents.

We signed him up for AFL (Australian Football) to give him a sense of belonging and a healthy way to be physical – to be active, an outlet for the emotions building up inside. We unfortunately didn't have anywhere for a punching bag or a gym. During this time we were given a dog, a story in itself because my hubby is not a dog person, but Ace became our boy's best friend and often knew that curling up on the bed, resting his head on him was what was needed, also meant a walking companion!

There were times it felt like we were walking on egg shells, scared to say the wrong thing that might tip him over the edge, the need to bleed affected the whole family, and sending the younger girls to their room didn't protect them as much as we hoped. We changed a saying: keep your friends close ... and your family closer.

The girls didn't need to know all the details but presenting them with a version of truth they could understand, to give them a framework of understanding, meant they weren't trying to make sense of things themselves and jumping to wrong conclusions. When we explained things to our middle girl she started crying and when I asked why, she thought her brother had cancer and was going to die.

At first, we tried to handle things on our own. I felt guilty. I felt I was failing. My husband couldn't get his head around it. It hurt him deeply too. What had we done wrong? ... but it wasn't about us. We realised to keep our son alive we needed help. We worked with a psychologist and the school was fantastic! We talked a lot about recognising the emotions that drove the need to bleed and set up other options, even developing a code word, so we knew without many words where he was at mentally.

It took months, and in times of stress he would fall back into this horrible habit. He still lives with the scars. Today he is the head merchandiser for a major hardware store. He is living out of home. He still has his low times, but he can pick it himself. He comes back home during these times for support.

Taking Care of Your Relationship

The stress associated with a young person going through a 'rough patch' of any kind can put a lot of pressure on a relationship. I have seen couples struggle under the pressure of looking after a child who self-harms. If partners aren't willing to *choose* to take care of each other, I wonder if it is possible to stay connected. Our marriages and relationships need to outlive self-harm but won't if we neglect them. I would actually suggest that couples deliberately talk about the future and happier things, as self-harm can easily become all consuming.

Collett Smart, psychologist who has worked with families for over 20 years, says, 'When we are under stress, our partners are often those closest to us that we have to lash out on – simply because we can. I think the first step in protecting our marriages is to recognise this fact. So sit down and talk about it and make the choice, together, to do your best not to hurt each other. Begin to see yourselves as part of the same team, because you both want your child to get help or to get well.'

Smart also mentions, 'A key to safeguarding your marriage lies in how couples manage any decision-making process, especially in terms of care for a child in this instance. It's not whether there will be pitfalls along the way, because you know there will be, it's in a couple's ability to communicate with each other cooperatively and with respect.' I agree this is key when managing the inevitable tension that crisis times cause.

I have literally just got off the phone to a mother who spoke to me about her daughter. The ongoing pressure of the attention-seeking behaviour, which has surfaced in self-harm, digital self-harm, lies and manipulation, has left her feeling drained and despondent. One of the most reassuring things that she said to me in the conversation is that she is looking forward to speaking to her husband before talking to her daughter again. 'We always make decisions together,' were the words that she used.

Some of the biggest mistakes I see couples make is not taking time to communicate and make decisions together. I also regularly saw one parent hide self-harm behaviour from the other parent, which never aided shared parenting or communication. Not seeking help together – or separately when necessary – and not taking time out from the pressure were big red flags that usually didn't end well.

Different views between partners also causes tension – for example, if one parent wants to control the situation more, but the other parent wants to show more support. The young person self-harming may also 'play off' their mother and father, leaving their parents feeling like piggy in the middle. It is possible that parents also feel like there is one partner to blame for the young person's behaviour. All things are important to take time to resolve.

The Financial Cost

Families often tell me about the financial toll that self-harm has taken on their lives. Medical bills (from doctors, psychologists, psychiatrists and other alternative therapies) mount up, as does time off work (often unpaid after all sick leave and holiday pay had been used by up taking young people to appointments). For families who work from home or run their own businesses, it is difficult to balance being accessible and making money that a family relies on.

When I mentored young people, I found that families were willing to travel up to two hours to get to The Youth Excel Centre. I found myself trying to talk people out of coming to see me, insisting that they didn't need to put their family under any further stress by travelling such a great distance. However, in many cases they insisted and I am grateful that I have made some lasting and beautiful relationships with such families. My point is that the time that people would invest into seeking out the right help for their young person has to take a toll of their family finances. Obviously finding the right service for self-harm is not easy or they would have found it find locally.

I mention all this to say this: we are not going to do our families any good by managing the immediate crisis and losing the end game. We all have limits, and so do our bank accounts. There are times when we need to have the courage to say 'no' to the urgent for the good of the overall family. These are very hard decisions to make.

Taking Care of Siblings

My mind often wanders to how siblings are coping with self-harm when I am sitting with a family who is telling their story. My concern is that siblings can be experiencing secondary trauma and even neglect that goes undetected or seems justifiable. Parents may also become over-protective of younger siblings, micromanaging their behaviour in fear that they will self-harm as well. This may well be suffocating for them.

This section is all about taking a minute to stop and think about each of your children. Siblings can feel responsible, embarrassed, tired, stressed, angry or neglected. It is easy to overlook these needs. I know you probably feel caught in the middle, trapped between what is important and urgent, but I want to make sure you are aware and responding to them too.

Collett Smart says, 'Children and teens display signs of stress in so many different ways, so it is important to be aware that even three different kids in one family might display their stress in completely different ways.'

These are some signs of stress Smart suggested parents should look out for:
- Withdrawing from the family, spending more time alone in their rooms, not wanting to come home or not wanting to do things with the family as they usually would
- Putting up walls acting like nothing is bothering them or becoming defensive if asked to talk about how they are feeling
- Acting out, having tantrums or outbursts of anger, or becoming more tearful, or getting into trouble at school
- Internalising and beginning to have nightmares, wetting their beds, or becoming more anxious or fearful. Children may not want to leave their sibling or parent to go out or to school

Concluding Thoughts

I would also like to suggest that self-harm, like any challenge, can bring a family together. Think of this as an opportunity to parent your child in a memorable and meaningful way. Taking time to have these important conversations is critical in showing young people that you are a strong and capable parent that they can rely on.

I don't think there is any better way to validate intense emotion than to read other people's stories. That is why I have endeavoured to finish this book with real-life stories from families who have walked the journey. They are raw and real and will resonate and reassure you better than any research ever will.

Key Insights from this Chapter

- Our marriages and relationships need to outlive self-harm but won't if we neglect them.
- I suggest that couples deliberately talk about the future and happier things, as self-harm can easily become all consuming.
- Some of the biggest mistakes I see couples make is not taking time to communicate and make decisions together.

- We are not going to do our families any good by managing the immediate crisis and losing the end game. We all have limits, and so do our bank accounts.
- There are times when we need to have the courage to say 'no' to the urgent for the good of the overall family. These are very hard decisions to make.
- Siblings can feel responsible, embarrassed, tired, stressed, angry or neglected. It is easy to overlook these needs.

10

Stories of Hope

One mum messaged me after I announced on social media that I was writing about self-harm. Both her children had self-harmed, so she was qualified to have an opinion on the subject. I could hear her excitement as she said, 'Michelle, I'm so relieved to see someone writing about self-harm, as it is not often something a parent is prepared for. I didn't know where to go or who to talk to when I discovered my son and daughter self-harming. It happens; we react. We reacted several times! I read your post and I was thrilled to hear someone was talking about this topic.'

I get the sense that parents don't know where to find help once they discover their child self-harming. That is why I hope this book fills a much needed space on family's bookcases. However, I know that families are looking for more than information. They are looking for hope. Without hope our hearts feel sick, lost and unable to keep going. With it, I am sure the human spirit can overcome almost anything.

I have dedicated this last chapter to real life stories from people who have made it through self-harm. These stories have meant so much to me as I have read them. I know each of these people personally, and I have appreciated their honest contribution to this book and its readers. If you have a child who is struggling right now, I hope you are reassured that tomorrow can look very different than today.

Eunice's Story

22 years old

Looking back on my days when my mental health was the lowest, I felt as if I needed something that I could lean on, to help me cope. Unfortunately for me when I was 13 I came to believe that my 'crutch' should be self-harm. I battled with self-harm for about four years. At first it had been my last resort to cope and then it became something I went to straight away. I struggled with a lot of changes in high school, friendships and eventually family sickness and my dad's death.

I first learnt about self-harm in Year 8 from school and friends. I remember thinking if other people thought it could help, surely it would help me. After a year of self-harm, I began building a tolerance to the pain. I needed to feel more to numb me from what was going on with my depression and anxiety. The thing about self-harming is that I felt so incredibly shameful of what I had done, but yet I wanted people who cared about me to see, or to dig, to ask if I was okay.

When my poor mother first found out she was confused, angry and upset. I remember the first few days she cried and asked how I could do that to myself. Within a month I had finally agreed to go to counselling, though I didn't think I needed it, and how could they help? They didn't understand. And to be honest, at first not many people did. I've dealt with a lot of counsellors and teachers who wanted to help but when they tried, it actually hurt me more. I got asked a lot of questions like, 'Why ruin your body?', 'Why are you hurting yourself over small problems?', 'You must think it's cool', 'I don't understand you kids these days.' All of these statements and questions made me feel worse, made me feel abnormal and worthless.

But I finally found a person who didn't poke or prod me with questions. The first time I met Michelle she asked me about *me*, my likes, my hobbies. We talked that whole hour about everything but my problems. It made a big difference for me. She also spent time with my mum. A lot of other counsellors blamed and even interrogated my mum. I knew that they did that and that actually hurt me a lot because it wasn't her fault. She already blamed herself. I cannot stress enough how much my mother and Michelle helped me through this. With their love, constant support and non-judgment. My journey has been a long one, and it's had plenty of ups and downs. I want people to know it's not always smooth sailing. I relapsed a few times, but it didn't mean I was getting worse again. With time the self-harm happened less, and then it stopped. Finally, I learnt to replace negative coping mechanisms with positive ones. As well as that, positive people helped.

I can happily say that self-harm is in the past for me and that I am constantly working towards a healthier and positive state of mind. I am now 22 and grateful I had adults who stuck by me in those hard years.

Courtney's Story

20 years old

When I was in grade 7, my parents divorced. Although I saw it coming, the trauma of the event triggered many years of depression, self-harm and disordered eating. Along with the struggles of adapting to a broken family, I was dealing with friendship drama, self-esteem issues, and I hated school.

I had so much pain and self hate built up within myself that I felt the only way to relieve it was to take it out on my body. At first it was just a few scratches, and then it became an addiction and the cuts got very deep. Before I knew it, I was harming myself every day, because it gave me just a few minutes relief of the mess that was inside of my head. I had cuts and scars covering my arms and legs, wearing long sleeves in the middle of summer to hide it. Luckily, my parents found out pretty early on, and sent me to a psychologist where I was diagnosed with severe depression and anxiety at the age of 14.

I continued to see my psychologist to keep my family happy, but I was still struggling. I was starting to lose friends, I became scarily thin from my eating disorder, and I didn't think I was going to make it to my 16 birthday. After a few attempted overdoses and very deep cuts that my mum found out about, she was worried sick and dragged me to the hospital against my will. I wasn't admitted because I convinced the doctors that I was fine, but truthfully that was the wake-up call I needed to seriously get help.

Finally, at the age of 18, I thought I had beaten my depression, celebrating one year self-harm free. But a year later, my depression had crept its way back in, and at the end of 2017 I found myself being rushed to hospital after another attempted suicide. It was there in that hospital room, at nearly 20 years old that I realised this was no longer the answer. I felt ashamed that I had let myself get to that point again, and I promised myself I would never hit that rock bottom again. With the support of friends, family and professionals, I made a pretty fast recovery and I can honestly say I feel like a new person with a new outlook on life.

Although it has taken me many long, hard years to battle this, I can finally say I'm on the road to recovery and I don't see myself turning back. I've now realised that my body should never have been the punching bag for my issues, and the pain that I used to find relief in no longer serves a purpose any more. Looking at my scars, I don't feel ashamed and I don't feel the need to hide them, but they are something I will have to live with for the rest of my life. Some days, I can't believe I'm still here, after everything I went through. But I remind myself every day that I am living proof of strength and resilience, and my past has made me who I am today.

Rachael's Story

Mother and student counsellor who has worked with self-harm for the past ten years.

My journey of using self-harm was something that started at around the age of 14 for me, and included a number of different methods from eating disordered behaviour (restricted eating, binging, and purging) through to cutting, and, most commonly, burning myself.

I grew up in a very loving and caring home with parents who loved me dearly; however emotions were a hard thing to display for me and my family – especially the difficult ones.

It wasn't until my early teenage years when some of the trauma from years of childhood sexual abuse began to really affect me. I found myself having nightmares, flashbacks, and lots of different emotions I wasn't sure how to deal with, or even put words to. This is when self-harm began to creep in – it helped to validate some of the shame and darkness that I felt inside. It gave words to things: memories and pains that I couldn't yet talk about. I was a young girl, crying out for help and attention in a world where she felt everything was falling apart and no one truly understood.

Self-harm was something that I would find myself turning to on and off throughout a number of years; when things got too much, when I didn't have the words, when everything felt overwhelming, I would find the temptation to want to hurt myself would creep back in. Even still to this day, if I'm having a really dark and hard time I still find that my thoughts can wander into that direction. But that's all it ever is these days: a thought.

Because I now know that the purpose that self-harm once served, and once had a time for, it no longer does. I know now that my body doesn't deserve the pain inflicted on it, and that the method of self-harm isn't a solution, only a temporary band-aid that causes more long-term issues. I now know that there are many other, healthier alternatives that I can turn to for comfort and release – that do not need to involve hurting my body, my mind, or my loved ones who helplessly look on. Teenage me couldn't yet comprehend this – but adult me knows that even in those times where I still feel speechless, and don't have the words to put to a broken past, self-harm is not and never will be the answer or what I need.

My body has many scars on it – physical and emotional. And they all tell a story. But now, it's a story of hope. That there once was a time that I too believed that my future didn't really hold anything ahead for me. That each day was a struggle and a fight. But now, I have the honour and privilege of sitting alongside young people on a daily basis and encouraging them that no matter what their past, there is ALWAYS hope for the future. And that healing and freedom isn't a destination, but a lifelong journey of new discoveries. There will be mountain top experiences, valley low experiences, and lots of in between places along the way – but as you look back you can be proud to say, 'Wow, look how far I have come, look at what I've learnt, and look at who I've helped and encouraged in their journeys! I may not be where I want to be yet – but I'm on my way and I'm going to take every moment of learning as I go!'

Jacob's Story

21 years old

At age 12 I started to hate school. The workload stressed me to the point of full-on panic. Bullying was coming and going. At 13, I was missing up to 60% of school because I would be terrified to show my face, due to either homework or assignments or even my issues with friends. At 14, I was diagnosed with anxiety and depression. I was struggling with day-to-day menial tasks from getting out of bed to getting dressed for school. At 15, I tried to take my life and started self-harming almost religiously. It's easily the lowest point of my life and it resulted in a stay in hospital for three months over the course of three years.

I wouldn't take back those months for anything. I learned a lot in my time on the ward, including what I wanted to do with my life and how to stay safe when I'm having a bad day, and I met some of the strongest, most tolerant and understanding people in the world. After my last visit in March 2016, I have not been admitted to a mental ward since and have been piecing my life back together slowly but surely and got up to one year clean of self-harm. I went through a mental health clinic for about a year and then I returned to my private psychologist and psychiatrist and continued to work through my safety plan and what was the best way to go about my recovery. Many tough calls had to be made and many habits and social ties had to be broken for my recovery.

There have been a few instances where I relapsed, and I did have to be taken to emergency after an OD (overdose) once. Looking back on it now that's all I see it as: a relapse. It didn't put me back to where I was five years ago. It only made me want to beat back these demons more. That was in 2017. Almost a year later I am back up to a year clean. It may be a strange thing to keep track of and I know it will be devastating if that streak was to be broken, but it is one of the biggest motivators I have and I have a support network to help me back it if that was to ever happen.

A few months ago my safety plan was tested, and it was probably one of the hardest tests I've gone through. I followed my plan and it succeeded in keeping me safe. Talking to people I trusted deeply is probably the reason I didn't fall back into a relapse.

My journey has been one of a kind, as it is any with mental illness. I have decided to use my experiences to help teens going through similar problems I went through just as my psychologist did for me. One of the things we loved to talk about was books, and one of the things that we would come back to is a particular thing in a specific book called *The Labyrinth.* Everyone goes through their own labyrinth at some point in their life. I look back on my labyrinth and see it as a learning experience, and one I can use to help those who are just starting their labyrinth.

Even though my journey has a way to go, I'm gonna fight to see it and help others fight to see their own. When I have helped people, whether it was stopping them from self-harming or suicide itself or just helping in general, it gave me a sense of relief. Relief that they were okay for at least a little longer and that they would know someone loved and cared for them. I am only 20 years old so I have a lot of life left to live and give.

Jen's story

40 years old

I am 40 and I live with the scars of tumultuous years of my youth. As a teenager and young adult I had raging emotions that I didn't know where they had come from or how to deal with them. I turned to many destructive behaviours as a means to nullify and numb the emotion as the intensity was beyond my capability to process – or at least I thought it was. I was also so tormented that to speak of any of this I felt that I would be misunderstood and further alienated. One of the ways I coped was to self-harm. I don't know how this really began and perhaps it was a learnt behaviour that I observed from other adolescents I was in hospital with at the time, but I realised it worked – or at least at the time I thought it did.

Initially the self-harm began as bashing walls or bashing my arms, then it progressed to a few superficial scratches but, as time passed, like any addiction the need and desire for relief meant I self-harmed more often and in most instances made cuts that were deep, needing suturing, including internal sutures. The depth of my despair and destructive behaviour hospitalised me on two occasions, requiring blood transfusions due to extreme blood loss.

To those around me I was attention seeking. But I wasn't. I would often hide what I had done, meaning many cuts went without treatment because I didn't want people to take away the only thing I felt I had to cope with the torment and torture I was experiencing. Self-harm was never about seeking attention. It was a cry for help and a means to show I was hurting to those who had eyes to see, ears to hear and a heart to understand. Furthermore, since I felt so unworthy of life and experiences that brought success and happiness, self-harm was a means to self-sabotage. In my late teens, early twenties, I commenced a hairdressing apprenticeship. I was doing well and enjoying life momentarily. Yet, since I didn't believe I deserved this, my self-harming ramped up and my goal was to do nerve or tendon damage to prevent any success in the field. Fortunately, this didn't happen.

Many people would say that when I was older I would look at my scars I had all over my body and regret it. At that time in my life I didn't care. I didn't want to make it to my next birthday let alone 40 years of age so what was a few scars going to matter? But here I am, 40! I am not proud of my scars, yet I am not ashamed of them. I am often asked about them but am not forthright in sharing. My scars are deeply personal. Whilst at the time I didn't understand or know why I was led to such destruction, in recovery I learnt it was a well-devised method to protect myself from dealing with extreme trauma and abuse. My scars are a constant reminder not of those ugly years in my life but a reminder of God's love and grace for me. They remind me of just what He has rescued me from. They remind me of the purpose I have and the beauty He saw in my life. In times of intense and raw emotion I find that my automatic default is to want to self-harm to numb this emotion, but I don't. I am able to sit in the emotion, see it for what it is and process it in healthy ways.

Shelley's Story

Mum of two teenage girls

We first learned that our older daughter was self-harming when she was 12 years old. She took a hot curling iron and applied it to her left forearm – four times. I remember being so angry at her; I just couldn't understand what would drive her to do something so stupid, that would literally scar her for life.

Despite the anger, I was afraid to ask if the blistering burns were painful; then I didn't believe her when she said 'no'. You would think that going through this once would have prepared me for my younger daughter. But just like before, I saw no warning signs outside of what you would expect from a teenager. She was moody; in an instant, she could go from being 'normal' to being enraged, then becoming silent and isolating herself in her room. I honestly didn't think anything of it until the day when a mood struck and, through a series of events that followed, we discovered her journal and found out that not only had she been cutting herself on the arm, but that she was suicidal ... with a plan to hang herself.

Again, anger emerged from me. So did annoyance and irritation that she was mimicking her older sister. My husband, however, felt terrible, gut-wrenching guilt and shame that we had failed as parents. Maybe it was my coping mechanism, but I didn't feel the same. Instead, I kept telling myself that we did the best we could with what we saw in our daughter. If we had known that she would become suicidal, we certainly would have done things differently.

Hindsight is always 20/20. The only way my husband and I managed to survive and have a glimmer of hope was to cling to our faith in God. I turned to our friends for prayers and I had to believe that there were lessons for our family in these dark and stressful times. What I know for sure is that I needed to completely surrender my control, have faith and to trust that love would conquer all.

Brianna's Story

20 years old

When I was 14 I was self-harming. There was a lot going on at home. My dad had just joined the army and had just been deployed. I starting home schooling and my uncle broke his leg and his whole family came to live with us. We had 7 new kids in the house, and mattresses all over the floor. I stepped up to help mum but didn't know how to process everything. I looked like I was on top of it but underneath I was not coping.

I got Instagram when I was 14. I actually got Instagram even before I got Facebook. We had a whole bunch of rules for Facebook in our house – we had to ask, etc. But my parents hadn't even heard of Instagram, so I didn't even think of asking them. My mum just thought it was a photo editing app.

I remember googling in a hash tag of anxiety and depression, and somehow came across this self-harm account. I started following it, and a whole tone more of them. At the time I thought I had found a community I could relate to. They understood what I was going through, and it made me feel normal. I really didn't want to put any more burden on my mum, so I did everything I could to deal with it myself.

The Instagram accounts I was following would coach me through self-harm. I would comment on something and they would be like 'me too' and reaffirm what I was thinking. It made me feel like I was doing okay. I followed them for ages.

After a year later I realised that what I was doing wasn't the healthiest thing in the world. There was this one account and that I had followed from the beginning. The girl was about 17 years-old. She posted about her self-harm every day.

She started wanting to get better at the same time I was. Then I found she was posting about her relapses. She would say, I'm having a good day. Then the next few days it would be-relapse, relapse, relapse ... Every time I saw her relapse it made me thinking about relapsing too.

Then overnight she changed the name of her account. Instead of "xx cutter" it became a positive self-care account. Every day she posted about loving yourself, going to counselling, the strategies that were helping her. She never spoke about relapsing again. It was a wake up moment for me. I decided to go through all my accounts and deleted all the other accounts that I was following.

I didn't go back to the self-harm accounts that often. I would have to go and search for them, and by the time I found them I was like, 'This is so silly what you are doing?" The internet had a positive and a negative impact on me when I was a teenager. I think it is really dangerous for kids, but I also see how if they look up to someone positive it can be a good thing too.

Andrew's Story
Aged 30

The tendency to be self-critical and self-loathing is something that developed over the course of my childhood. My parents' words had a great deal to do with the way I saw myself and my capacity to handle the pressures of life. I remember doing a project about dinosaurs in primary school and my mother called me 'stupid' as she often did. I was nine at the time. Moments like these had a big impact on me.

My parents had their own baggage they were dealing with, as all parents do. We didn't have a lot growing up. They were two very emotional people. Things would build up and there was a lot of yelling and tension in our house. Whenever I did something 'wrong', aggression was the way they dealt with it.

By my early teen years I felt like there was so much in my life which was out of control. Friendship were constantly changing for me as we moved around a lot. I was always trying to re-establish friendships, which was hard. There were times when my friends were really nasty. Being a gentle soul, it was easy to feel hurt by other people's stronger personalities.

I started to smoke and drink in high school as a way of fitting in. My parents didn't know. They would be at work while I was at home getting smashed. I didn't seem to know when to stop and how to care for myself. When I was in my late teen years I started experimenting with drugs. I ended up telling my parents because I wanted a clear conscience.

I grew up in the bush where it was common for people to have guns. My father had a gun which he had since his own childhood. There were many times throughout my teen years that I loaded my father's gun, sat on his bed and starred down it's barrel. This was very secretive behaviour that my parents didn't know about. I was alone with the gun and my thoughts. There were numerous times I was so close to pulling the trigger. There were also times that I took a knife and dreamed about pushing it into my chest.

I was randomly sexually assaulted by a guy in a public pool when I was 12. He was a stranger, but I had to go and do a police report. That was a big thing for me as a young boy. I would regularly have nightmares about him climbing through my window. When I was in Year 9, I mentioned it to a classmate, who made a big deal about it in class. It became a teasing point and the teacher didn't do anything to stop it. I felt like my whole world was imploding.

My parents were oblivious to what I was feeling. They didn't understand me, and I couldn't relate and express myself to them. During high school I tried to overdose on Panadol. I broke 24 of them and turned them into a paste. I was actually mixing this concoction at the kitchen table while my father was watching TV in the other room. He was dealing with a lot of his own stress, so he was pretty disengaged with me at the time. I never ended up in hospital or went to a doctor, but I did get really sick!

I never spoke to anyone about what I was thinking or feeling – at home or school. To be fair, no one actually asked either. I turned to poetry (dark poetry) which no one ever found. For me depression was like I was in a hole that I couldn't get out of.

I wish all parents could keep reflecting, growing and learning. Both my parents grew up with abusive fathers. I am sure they thought they were doing the best that they could do. It just shows how easy it is for kids to hide where they are at and how diligent patents need to be in order to stay connected to them.

It is not until you can reflect back later that you can determine that your behaviour was self-harm. It is only later that I can see the signs and patterns that trapped me. Back then, I would self-harm to make myself feel good. Hurting myself brought me joy. It's a big thing to say that, but it is true.

When I moved to the city it helped me. We had more people around us and build a community that actually helped support my family. The friends I made in the city were more positive. I started to take responsibility for my future. Smoking and alcohol disappeared from my life. That made a big difference to my health and strength mentally. I married a girl who has helped me immensely. I'd actually say she is the reason I am so strong now.

I'd like every parent to realise that children want to connect (and be connected) to their parents. They need their parents to be parents and have the wisdom and the knowledge to reach out and build bridges.

They don't want to feel like their parents are disappointed with them (or too busy or preoccupied to seek the truth out). Disappointment reinforces negative thinking and perpetuates the cycle of depression. In my lowest moments I didn't feel loved. I felt guilt and disappointment, which made me want to self-harm more.

If you have a child who is self-harming, it doesn't matter how many times it takes to reach out to them. You just have to keep trying. At the end of the day you are either going to help them get through the fog of what they are experiencing, or you are leaving them to try and navigate it for themselves.

Looking Forward with Hope

If you are a parent who is caring for a child who is self-harming, I would like to leave you with these final words. No one anticipates that their child will self-harm. The unexpected road that you have found yourself walking down may seem overwhelming, long and difficult. You may feel isolated and lonely, travelling a path that few others understand.

Regardless of how tired or drained you may feel right now, I want to ask you to never stop believing that tomorrow can be better. Hope is something that you need to cling onto with every ounce of strength that you have. Never let it go, and never let anyone steal it from you; not even your child who may not be able to see the light at the end of their dark tunnel. When a child doesn't have the eyes to see a bright future, a parent's love sees it for them.

Acknowledgements

A book like this doesn't just happen without a team of people who are dedicated to its message.

I would firstly like to thank my team at Big Sky Publishing for so enthusiastically getting behind this book. Your sincere dedication to helping families has meant the world to me. I can't thank you enough for your genuine interest in my work.

To Di, my publishing manager-I need to send a very big, special thank you to you. Thank you for attending to my endless emails, and nervous moments. You have been so patient with my creativity and so careful with this book's development. There is no one else I would have rather worked with. Thank you also to Jane, who edited my work with such understanding of who I am; Sharon, whose creative eye and marketing skills are an author's dream; and Chris, for his attention to detail on the book's graphics. Without you this book would not be possible.

I want to thank every single professional, school and parent who has prodded me to write this book. It's a big topic to tackle and one which I have been cautious approaching. Thank you for alerting me to the need, and for taking me on a heart wrenching journey which has opened my eyes to what children (and parents of children) who self-harm go through.

Thank you to Generation Next who first gave me the platform to share my work in this area, and The Resilient Kids Conference for embracing it. I appreciate your willingness to get this message to families who need it.

Thank you also the families who have shared their deeply personal stories in this book. Your bravery and desire to help others inspires me. I know that a resource like this would have made a huge difference during your hardest times, so thank you for lightening the load for others. Although names have been changed or omitted to protect privacy, I still recognise that seeing your family's story in print is something many wouldn't sign up for.

A special thanks to my personal clients (some who I hadn't seen for fifteen years). The fact that we were able to reunite to work on this is something I am truly grateful for. My relationship with you means a great deal to me. You teach me a great deal about courage and persistence. Your stories have shed light on an often misunderstood topic and I hope their impact will go far and wide.

Thank you also to expert's Dr Sameer Hinduja, Maggie Dent, Collette Smart and Susan McLean who have offered their expertise to this delicate topic. I greatly respect your work and thank you for all you do for families. You are paving the way for healthier families in this nation and across the world which is no small feat.

I was very lucky to have so many schools willing to talk to me about this topic. Thank you to the principals, teachers, guidance officers and student support staff who shared their experiences and thoughts. Rachael Rubio and Louise Klar, your ongoing relationship is a blessing to me. Your grassroots approach is always good value and one which needs to be shared.

I would like to specifically thank Rob Micklewright, a long term friend and tech extraordinaire who spent loads of time talking to me about digital self-harm and the tech space. Thank you also to Carl Hotko, Jane Webber, Renee Bennett and Annette Spur for their interviews and interest in children's online safety and mental health.

Lastly, I would like to thank my family who are always involved in my work in some way — even if it is because my office is near the kitchen and they interrupt my writing to be fed!

Ben, your intelligence and logic are something I respect, as you know. Thank you for questioning me, helping me interpret research and medical lingo, and contributing your ideas at crazy times of the day and night. You help me far more than you know. Matt, thank you for being my emergency camera man and encouraging me to be an Instagram sensation. I am so proud of both of you and your heart to help others.

To my husband, who is my greatest (and loudest) cheer squat. I know you will always believe in me. Thank you for supporting me while writing this book, buying me flowers for my desk, squeezing in the occasional edit and telling me my work is fabulous even when I don't think it is. Thank you for encouraging me to keep going when I don't think I can. Your friendship means the world to me.

And finally to my parents, Alan and Pat. Mum, you are the best editor in the world. No one can edit like a mum! There are few errors that get past you, even at 12pm at night. Thank you for tirelessly helping your children and being such a great role model for me. Dad, thanks for the coffee and omelettes, and for always inspiring me to love other people. I take after you. xx

Resources and Websites

Remember help is only a decision away. If you are looking for more support, here are some further resources I can recommend.

Help Lines:

Lifeline Australia – 13 11 14
Life Line Text-tel: 0477 13 11 14
Suicide Call Back Service – 1300 659 467
Kids Helpline Australia – 1800 55 1800
Kids Matter: 1800 55 180
SANE Australia: 1800 187 263
Youth beyondblue – 1300 22 4636
Headspace Australia – 1800 650 890

Support Services:

Royal Australian and New Zealand College of Psychiatry: www.ranzcp.org

Australian Association of Psychologists – www.aapoz.com

Australian Psychological Association: www.psychology.org.au

Australian Counselling Association: www.theaca.net.au

Headspace: www.headspace.org.au

COPMI (Children of Parents with Mental Illness): www.copmi.net.au

Parentline: www.parentline.com.au

Useful Apps:

#selfcare
Calm Harm
Mood Path
The Breathing APP
Sleep Cycle
Smiling Mind

The Resilience Project
Headspace: Guided Meditation
30-Day Gratitude Challenge

Recommended Reading:

Check out Michelle's Accompanying Resource-*Everyday Resilience: Helping Kids Handle Friendship Drama, Academic Pressure and the Self-Doubt of Growing Up.*

This book is dedicated to preventing self-harm and building resilience in young people.

About the Author

Michelle is an award-winning speaker, author and educator whose passion is to support families.

Michelle started her career as a teacher. In 2000 Michelle left teaching and founded Youth Excel, a charity which has supported thousands of young people and their families with life skills education, mentoring and psychological services.

Michelle's hands-on experience and passion for 'all things young people' has made her a sought-after and entertaining speaker. She has a unique ability to transfer years of knowledge to a wide range of audiences.

Michelle's innovative work has been featured on the TODAY Show, Channel Ten Morning News, Today Tonight, 96fivefm, ABC radio and in countless print media including The Age, Australian Women's Weekly and the Courier Mail.

Michelle is the author of four books, and the co-author of one – *What Teenage Girls Don't Tell their Parents,*

Parenting Teenage Girls is the Age of a New Normal and *Everyday Resilience: Helping Kids Handle Friendship Drama, Academic Pressure and the Self-Doubt of Growing Up.* She is the co-author of *Raising Resilient Kids.*

Michelle's books and resources have been called a 'guiding light' for parents and professionals. She has a marvellous way of speaking truth in a way that all appreciate.

She lives in Brisbane with her husband and two teenagers.
Find out more:
www.michellemitchell.org
Facebook: Michelle Mitchell – Author, Speaker, Educator
Instagram: @michellemitchellspeaker

Endnotes

A Quick Definition

The National Suicide Research Foundation, 'The National Self-Harm Registry Ireland,' [Online]. Available: https://www.nsrf.ie/our-research/our-systems/national-self-harm-registry-ireland/. (Accessed October 2018).

Kidger J, Heron J, Lewis G, Evans J and Gunnell D, 2012, 'Adolescent self-harm and suicidal thoughts in the ALSPAC cohort: a self-report survey in England', *BMC Psychiatry,* vol.12, no.69.

Scoliers G, Portzyky G, Madge N, Hewitt A, Hawton K, de Wilde E J, Ystgaard M, Arensman E, De Leo D, Fekete S and van Heeringen K, 2008, 'Reasons for adolescent deliberate self-harm: A cry of pain and/or a cry for help? Findings from the child and adolescent self-harm in Europe (CASE) study,' *Soc Psychiatry Psychiatr Epidemiol,* vol.44, no.8, pp.601-7.

Why I Wrote This Book

Chandler A, 2017, 'Seeking Secrety: A Qualitative Study of Younger Adolesecents' Accounts of Self-Harm', *SAGE Publications,* vol.26, no.4, pp.313–331.

Klonsky D, 2009, 'The functions of self-injury in young adults who cut themselves, clarifying the evidence for affect regulation,' *Psychiatry Res,* vol.166, no.2-3, pp.260-8.

Chapter 1-The Important Basics

This chapter draws on a composite of resources, including:

Barrocas A, Hankin B L, Young J, Abela J.R.Z, 2012, 'Rates of Non-Suicidal Self-Injury in Youth: Age, Sex, and Behavioral Methods in a Community Sample', The American Academy of Pediatrics.

Fields H, 2004, 'State dependent opioid control of pain,' *Nature Reviews Neuroscience,* vol.5, pp.565-75.

Griffin E, McMahon E, McNicholas F, Corcoran P, Perry I J and Arensman E,

2018, 'Increasing rates of self-harm amongst children, adolescents and young adults: a 10-year national registry study 2007-2016,' *Social Psychiatry Psychiatr Epidemiol,* vol.53, no.7, pp.663-671.

Kelly B D, 2018, 'Are we finally making progress with suicide and self-harm? An overview of the history, epidemiology and evidence for prevention', *Irish Journal of Psychological Medicine,* vol.35, pp.95–101.

Kidger J, Heron J, Lewis G, Evans J and Gunnell D, 2012, 'Adolescent self-harm and suicidal thoughts in the ALSPAC cohort: a self-report survey in England', *BMC Psychiatry,* vol.12, no.69.

Klonsky D, 2009, 'The functions of self-injury in young adults who cut themselves, clarifying the evidence for affect regulation,' *Psychiatry Res,* vol.166, no.2-3, pp.260-8.

Lawrence D, Johnson S, Hafekost J, Boterhoven de Haan, K Ainley J, Sawyer M and Zubrick S R, 2015, 'The Mental Health of Children and Adolescents: Report on the second Australian child and adolescent survey of mental health and wellbeing,' The Department of Health, Canberra.

Levesque R J R, 2010, 'Special Issue Introduction: the place of self-harm in adolescent development,' *J Youth Adolesc,* vol.39, no.3, pp.217-8.

Liu R T, 2017, 'Characterising the course of non-suicidal self-injury: A cognitive neuroscience perspective,' *Neurosci Biobehav Rev,* vol.80, p.159-65, Sep.2017.

Madge N, Hewitt A, Hawton K, de Wilde E J, Corcoran P, Fekete S, van Heeringen K de Leo D and Ystgaard M, 2008, 'Deliberate self-harm within an international community sample of young people: comparative findings from the Child & Adolescent Self-harm in Europe (CASE) study,' *J Child Psychol Psychiatry,* vol.49, no.6, p.667-77.

Madge, N, Hawton K, McMahon E, Corcoran P, de Leo D, de Wilde E J, Fekete S, van Heeringen K, Ystgaard M and Arensman E, 2011, 'Psychological characteristics, stressful life events and deliberate self-harm: findings from the Child and Adolescent Self-Harm in

Europe (CASE) Study,' *Eur Child Adolesc Psychiatry,* vol.20, no.10, pp.498-508.

McMahon M, O'Regan G, Corcoran P, Arensman E, Cannon M, Williamson E, Keeley H, 'Young Lives in Ireland: A school-based study of mental health and suicide prevention', 2017, National Research Foundation.

Mission Australia, 2017, 'Youth Mental Health Report: Youth Survey 2012-2016,' Mission Australia and Black Dog Institute, Sydney.

Moreno M A, Ton A, Selkie E and Evans Y, 2016, 'Secret Society 123: Understanding the Language of Self-Harm on Instagram,' *J Adolesc Health,* vol.58, no.1, pp.78-84.

Psych Central, [Online]. Available: https://psychcentral.com/disorders/. (Accessed: October 2018)

Scoliers G, Portzyky G, Madge N, Hewitt A, Hawton K, de Wilde E J, Ystgaard M, Arensman E, De Leo D, Fekete S and van Heeringen K, 2008, 'Reasons for adolescent deliberate self-harm: A cry of pain and/or a cry for help? Findings from the child and adolescent self-harm in Europe (CASE) study,' *Soc Psychiatry Psychiatr Epidemiol,* vol.44, no.8, pp.601-7.

Someah K, 2012 'Common Self-Harm Behaviours', [Online]. Eating Disorder Hope, Available: https://www.eatingdisorderhope.com/treatment-for-eating-disorders/co-occurring-dual-diagnosis/self-injury/self-harm-as-a-co-occurring-issue-of-eating-disorders, (Accessed September 2018).

The National Collaborating Centre for Mental Health, 2004, 'Self-harm: The short-term physical and psychological management and secondary prevention of self-harm in primary and secondary care', The British Psychological Society and The Royal College of Psychiatrists.

The National Suicidal Research Foundation, 2016, 'Northern Ireland Registry of Self-Harm: Regional Three-Year Report, 2012/13 to 2014/15', [Online] Available: http://www.publichealth.hscni.net/publications/northern-ireland-registry-self-harm-three-year-report-201213-201415 (Accessed October 2018)

The National Suicide Research Foundation, 'The National Self-Harm Registry Ireland,' [Online]. Available: h ttps://www.nsrf.ie/our-research/our-systems/national-self-harm-registry-ireland/. (Accessed October 2018).

Townsend E, Wadman R, Sayal K, Armstrong M, Harroe C, Majumder P, Vostains P, Clarke D, 'Uncovering key patterns in self-harm in adolescents: Sequences analysis using the Card Sort Task for Self-harm (CaTS)', 2016, *Journal of Affective Disorders,* Volume 206, pp.161–168.

Zetterqvist M, Svedin C G, Fredlund C, Priebe G, Wadsby M, Johnsson L S, 2018, 'Self-reported nonsuicidal self-injury (NSSI) and sex as a self-injury (SASI): Relationship to abuse, risk behaviors, trauma symptoms, self-esteem and attachment', *Psychiatry Research,* p.309–316.

Chapter 2-The Psychology and Physiology

This chapter draws on a composite of resources, including:

Ballard E, Bosk A, Pao M, 2010, 'Invited Commentary: Understanding Brain Mechanisms of Pain Processing in

Adolescents' Non-Suicidal Self-Injury', *J Youth Adolescence,* vol.39, pp.327-334.

Brent D A and Mann J J, 2006, 'Familial Pathways to Suicidal Behaviour: understanding and preventing suicide among adolescents,' *N Engl J Med,* vol.355, no.28, pp.2719-21.

Bridge J A, Goldstein T R, Brent D A, 2006, 'Adolescent Suicide and Suicidal Behaviour,' *J Child Psychol Psychiatry,* vol.47, no.3-4, pp.372-94.

Fields H, 2004, 'State dependent opioid control of pain,' Nature Reviews Neuroscience, vol.5, pp.565-75.

Griffin E, McMahon E, McNicholas F, Corcoran P, Perry I J and Arensman E, 2018 'Increasing rates of self-harm amongst children, adolescents and young adults: a 10-year national registry study 2007-2016,' *Soc Psychiatry Psychiatr Epidemiol,* vol.53, no.7, pp.663-671.

Hawton K, Saunders K E and O'Connor R C, 2012, 'Self Harm and suicide in adolescents,' *The Lancet,* vol.379, no.9834, pp.2317-82.

Kirtley O J, O'Carroll R E, O'Connor R E, 2016 'Pain and self-harm: A systematic review', *Journal of Affective Disorders,* vol.203, pp.347-363.

Klonsky D, 2009, 'The functions of self-injury in young adults who cut themselves, clarifying the evidence for affect regulation,' *Psychiatry Res,* vol.166, no.2-3, pp.260-8.

Liu R T, 2017, 'Characterising the course of non-suicidal self-injury: A cognitive neuroscience perspective,' *Neurosci Biobehav Rev,* vol.80, p.159-65, Sep.2017.

Madge N, Hewitt A, Hawton K, de Wilde E J, Corcoran P, Fekete S, van Heeringen K de Leo D and Ystgaard M, 2008, 'Deliberate self-harm within an international community sample of young people: comparative findings from the Child & Adolescent Self-harm in Europe (CASE) study,' *J Child Psychol Psychiatry,* vol.49, no.6, p.667-77.

Melham N M, Day N, Shear M K, Day R, Reynolds C F, Brent D, 2004, 'Traumatic Grief Among Adolescents exposed to a peer's suicide,' *Am J Psychiatry,* vol.161, no.8, pp.1411-6.

Mission Australia, 2017, 'Youth Mental Health Report: Youth Survey

2012-2016,' Mission Australia and Black Dog Institute, Sydney.

Nestler E J, Hyman S E and Malenka R, 2010, *Molecular Neuropharmacology,* New York: McGraw-Hill Medical.

Stanley B, Sher L, Wilson S, Ekman R, Huang Y Y and Mann J J, 2010, 'Non-suicidal self-injurious behavior, endogenous opioids and monoamine neurotransmitters,' *J. Affect Disord.,* vol.224, no.1-2, pp.134-40.

Chapter 3 – The Role of the Internet

This chapter draws on a composite of resources, including:

Baker N, 2018, 'Self-harm amongst youth surges 22%', *Irish Examiner,* [Online] Available at: https://www.irish examiner.com/ireland/self-harm-among-youth-surges-22-471021.html

Chandler A, 2017, 'Seeking Secrety: A Qualitative Study of Younger Adolesecents' Accounts of Self-Harm', *SAGE Publications,* vol.26, no.4, pp.313–331.

Jacob N, Evans R and Scourfield J, 2017, 'The influence of online images on self-harm: A qualitative study of young people aged 16-24,' *J Adolesc,* vol.60, pp.140-7.

Miguel E M, Chou T, Golik A, Cornacchino M S, Sanchez A, DeSerisy M, Comer J S, 'Examining the scope and patterns of deliberate self-injurious cutting content in popular social media', 2017, *Wiley Periodicals,* vol.34, pp.786–793.

Mission Australia, 2017, 'Youth Mental Health Report: Youth Survey 2012-2016,' Mission Australia and Black Dog Institute, Sydney.

Patchin J W and Hinduja S, 2017, 'Digital Self-Harm Among Adolescents,' *J Adolesc Health,* pp.761-6.

Chapter 4 – Digital Self-harm

This chapter draws on a composite of resources, including:

Englander E, 2012, 'Digital Self-Harm: Frequency, Type, Motivations, and Outcomes,' MARC Aggression Reduction Centre, [Online]. Available: http://vc.bridgew.edu/marc/D

IGITAL%20harm%20report.pdf [Accessed October 10, 2018]

Haines-Saah R J, Hilario C T, Jenkins E K, Ng C K Yand Johnson J L, 2016, 'Understanding adolescent narratives about "bullying" through an intersectional lens: Implications for Youth Mental Health Interventions,' *Youth & Society,* vol.50, no.5, pp.636-58.

Moreno M.A, Ton A, Selkie E, Evans Y, 'Secret Society 123: Understanding the Language of Self-Harm on Instagram', *Journal of Adolescent Health,* 2016, p 78–84.

Patchin J W and Hinduja S, 2017, 'Digital Self-Harm Among Adolescents,' *J Adolesc Health,* pp.761-6.

Weller C, 'A surprising number of teenagers are engaging in "digital self-harm,"' the practice of being mean to yourself online' [Online]. Business Insider Australia, Available: https://www.businessinsider.com.au/digital-self-harm-becoming-more-popular-among-teenagers-study-finds-2017-10?r=US&IR=T, [Accessed: Oct 10, 2018]

Chapter 5 – Must-have Conversations

This chapter draws on a composite of resources, including:

Bateman A, 'Self-harm', 2016. Royal College of Psychiatrists, [Online]. Available: https://www.rcpsych.ac.uk/mental-health/problems-disorders/self-harm (Accessed October 1, 2018)

Ferrey A E, Hughes N D, Simkin S, Locock L, Stewart A, Kapur N, Gunnell D and Hawton K, 2016, 'Changes in parenting strategies after a young person's self-harm: a qualitative study,' *Child Adolesc Psychiatry Ment Health*, vol.10.

Ferrey A E, Hughes N D, Simkin S, Locock L, Stewart A, Kapur N, Gunnell D, Hawton K, 2016, 'The impact of self-harm by young people on parents and families: a qualitative study,' *BMJ Open*, vol.6, no.1.

Klonsky D, 2009, 'The functions of self-injury in young adults who cut themselves, clarifying the evidence for affect regulation,' *Psychiatry Res*, vol.166, no.2-3, pp.260-8.

Chapter 6 – The Role of Professional Support and Schools

This chapter draws on a composite of resources, including:

Hodgkins S, 2016 'Positive Focus: A groupwork approach', London and New York, Routledge Taylor and Francis Group.

Law G. U, Rostill-Brookes H, Goodman D, 'Public stigma in health and non-healthcare students: Attributions, emotions and willingness to help with adolescent self-harm', 2009, *International Journal of Nursing Studies,* vol.46, pp.108–119.

Mitchell R, Seah R, Ting P H, Curtis K, Foster K, 2018, 'Intentional self-harm and assault hospitalisations and treatment cost of children in Australia over a ten year period', *Australian and New Zealand Journal of Public Health,* vol 42, pp.240-246.

National Collaborating Centre for Mental Health, 2004, 'Self-harm: The short-term physical and psychological management and secondary prevention of self-harm in primary and secondary care', The British Psychological Society and The Royal College of Psychiatrists.

Nearchou F A, Bird N, Costello A, Duggan S, Gilroy J, Long R, McHugh L and Hennessy E, 2018 'Personal and perceived public mental-health stigma as predictors of help-seeking intentions in adolescents,' *J Adolesc,* vol.66, pp.83-90.

Wester K L, Trepal H C, 2017 'Non-Suicidal Self-Injury: Wellness Perspectives on Behaviours, Symptoms and Diagnosis', London and New York, Routledge Taylor and Francis Group.

Chapter 7 – Self-Care and Safety Plans

This chapter draws on a composite of resources, including:

Klonsky D, 2009, 'The functions of self-injury in young adults who cut themselves, clarifying the evidence for affect regulation,' *Psychiatry Res,* vol.166, no.2-3, pp.260-8.

Levesque R J R, 2010, 'Special Issue Introduction: the place of self-harm in adolescent development,' *J Youth Adolesc,* vol.39, no.3, pp.217-8.

Mental Health First Aid Australia, Revised 2016, 'Suicidal Thoughts and Safety Plans: Mental Health First Aid Guidelines',. (Online) Accessible: https://mhfa.com.au/sites/default/files/MHFA_suicide_guidelinesA4%202014%20Revised.pdf Sited: November 2018.

Vivyan C, 'Get.gg,' 2011. [Online]. Available: https://www.getselfhelp.co.uk/docs/3Ds.pdf (Accessed Oct 10, 2018).

Chapter 8 – Parent as Coach

This chapter draws on a composite of resources, including:

Emmons R A, 2007, Thanks!: How the New Science of Gratitude Can Make You Happier, Boston: Houghton Mifflin Books

Hall K, 'Create a Sense of Belonging,' [Online]. Psychology Today, Available: https://www.psychologytoday.com/au/blog/pieces-mind/201403/create-sense-belonging (Accessed Oct 10, 2018).

Madge N, Hawton K, McMahon E, Corcoran P, de Leo D, de Wilde E J, Fekete S, van Heeringen K, Ystgaard M and Arensman E, 2011, 'Psychological characteristics, stressful life events and deliberate self-harm: findings from the Child and Adolescent Self-Harm in Europe (CASE) Study,' *Eur Child Adolesc Psychiatry,* vol.20, no.10, pp.498-508.

Madge N, Hewitt A, Hawton K, de Wilde E J, Corcoran P, Fekete S, van Heeringen K de Leo D and Ystgaard M, 2008, 'Deliberate self-harm within an international community sample of young people: comparative findings from the Child & Adolescent Self-harm in Europe (CASE) study,' *J Child Psychol Psychiatry,* vol.49, no.6, p.667-77.

Michelson D. Bhugra D., 'Family environment, expressed emotion and adolescent self-harm: A review of conceptual, empirical, cross-cultural and clinical perspectives' *International Review of Psychiatry,* April 2012; volume 24, p 106–114.

Chapter 9 – Taking Care of Family

This chapter draws on a composite of resources, including:

Emmons R A, 2007, Thanks!: How the New Science of Gratitude Can Make You Happier, Boston: Houghton Mifflin Books

Ferrey A E, Hughes N D, Simkin S, Locock L, Stewart A, Kapur N, Gunnell D and Hawton K, 2016, 'Changes in parenting strategies after a young person's self-harm: a qualitative study,' *Child Adolesc Psychiatry Ment Health*, vol.10.

Ferrey A E, Hughes N D, Simkin S, Locock L, Stewart A, Kapur N, Gunnell D, Hawton K, 2016, 'The impact of self-harm by young people on parents and families: a qualitative study,' *BMJ Open*, vol.6, no.1.

Hall K, 'Create a Sense of Belonging,' [Online]. *Psychology Today*, Available: https://www.psychologytoday.com/au/blog/pieces-mind/201403/create-sense-belonging (Accessed Oct 10, 2018).

Reference List

Baker N, 2018, 'Self-harm amongst youth surges 22%', *Irish Examiner,* [Online] Available at: https://www.irishexaminer.com/ireland/self-harm-among-youth-surges-22-471021.html

Ballard E, Bosk A, Pao M, 2010, 'Invited Commentary: Understanding Brain Mechanisms of Pain Processing in Adolescents' Non-Suicidal Self-Injury', *J Youth Adolescence,* vol.39, pp.327–334.

Barrocas A, Hankin B L, Young J, Abela J.R.Z, 2012, 'Rates of Non-Suicidal Self-Injury in Youth: Age, Sex, and Behavioral Methods in a Community Sample', The American Academy of Pediatrics.

Bateman A, 'Self-harm', 2016. Royal College of Psychiatrists, [Online]. Available: https://www.rcpsych.ac.uk/mental-health/problems-disorders/self-harm (Accessed October 1, 2018)

Brent D A and Mann J J, 2006, 'Familial Pathways to Suicidal Behaviour: understanding and preventing suicide among adolescents,' *N Engl J Med,* vol.355, no.28, pp.2719-21.

Bridge J A, Goldstein T R, Brent D A, 2006, 'Adolescent Suicide and Suicidal Behaviour,' *J Child Psychol Psychiatry,* vol.47, no.3-4, pp.372-94.

Chandler A, 2017, 'Seeking Secrety: A Qualitative Study of Younger Adolesecents' Accounts of Self-Harm', *SAGE Publications,* vol.26, no.4, pp.313–331.

Emmons R A, 2007, Thanks!: How the New Science of Gratitude Can Make You Happier, Boston: Houghton Mifflin Books

Englander E, 2012, 'Digital Self-Harm: Frequency, Type, Motivations, and Outcomes,' MARC Aggression Reduction Centre, [Online]. Available: http://vc.bridgew.edu/marc/DIGITAL%20harm%20report.pdf [Accessed October 10, 2018]

Ferrey A E, Hughes N D, Simkin S, Locock L, Stewart A, Kapur N, Gunnell D and Hawton K, 2016, 'Changes in parenting strategies after a young person's self-harm: a qualitative study,' *Child Adolesc Psychiatry Ment Health,* vol.10.

Ferrey A E, Hughes N D, Simkin S, Locock L, Stewart A, Kapur N, Gunnell

D, Hawton K, 2016, 'The impact of self-harm by young people on parents and families: a qualitative study,' *BMJ Open,* vol.6, no.1.

Fields H, 2004, 'State dependent opioid control of pain,' *Nature Reviews Neuroscience,* vol.5, pp.565-75.

Griffin E, McMahon E, McNicholas F, Corcoran P, Perry I J and Arensman E, 2018, 'Increasing rates of self-harm amongst children, adolescents and young adults: a 10-year national registry study 2007-2016,' *Social Psychiatry Psychiatr Epidemiol,* vol.53, no.7, pp.663-671.

Haines-Saah R J, Hilario C T, Jenkins E K, Ng C K Yand Johnson J L, 2016, 'Understanding adolescent narratives about "bullying" through an intersectional lens: Implications for Youth Mental Health Interventions,' *Youth & Society,* vol.50, no.5, pp.636-58.

Hall K, 'Create a Sense of Belonging,' [Online]. Psychology Today, Available: https://www.psychologytoday.com/au/blog/pieces-mind/201403/create-sense-belonging (Accessed Oct 10, 2018).

Hawton K, Saunders K E and O'Connor R C, 2012, 'Self Harm and suicide in adolescents,' *The Lancet,* vol.379, no.9834, pp.2317-82.

Hodgkins S, 2016 'Positive Focus: A groupwork approach', London and New York, Routledge Taylor and Francis Group.

Jacob N, Evans R and Scourfield J, 2017, 'The influence of online images on self-harm: A qualitative study of young people aged 16-24,' *J Adolesc,* vol.60, pp.140-7.

Kelly B D, 2018, 'Are we finally making progress with suicide and self-harm? An overview of the history, epidemiology and evidence for prevention', *Irish Journal of Psychological Medicine,* vol.35, pp.95–101.

Kidger J, Heron J, Lewis G, Evans J and Gunnell D, 2012, 'Adolescent self-harm and suicidal thoughts in the ALSPAC cohort: a self-report survey in England', *BMC Psychiatry,* vol.12, no.69.

Kirtley O J, O'Carroll R E, O'Connor R E, 2016 'Pain and self-harm: A systematic review', *Journal of Affective Disorders,* vol.203, pp.347–363.

Klonsky D, 2009, 'The functions of self-injury in young adults who cut themselves, clarifying the evidence for affect regulation,' *Psychiatry Res,* vol.166, no.2-3, pp.260-8.

Law G. U, Rostill-Brookes H, Goodman D, 'Public stigma in health and non-healthcare students: Attributions, emotions and willingness to help with adolescent self-harm', 2009, *International Journal of Nursing Studies,* vol.46, pp.108–119.

Lawrence D, Johnson S, Hafekost J, Boterhoven de Haan, K Ainley J, Sawyer M and Zubrick S R, 2015, 'The Mental Health of Children and Adolescents: Report on the second Australian child and adolescent survey of mental health and wellbeing,' The Department of Health, Canberra.

Levesque R J R, 2010, 'Special Issue Introduction: the place of self-harm in adolescent development,' *J Youth Adolesc,* vol.39, no.3, pp.217-8.

Liu R T, 2017, 'Characterising the course of non-suicidal self-injury: A cognitive neuroscience perspective,' *Neurosci Biobehav Rev,* vol.80, p.159-65, Sep.2017.

Madge N, Hawton K, McMahon E, Corcoran P, de Leo D, de Wilde E J, Fekete S, van Heeringen K, Ystgaard M and Arensman E, 2011, 'Psychological characteristics, stressful life events and deliberate self-harm: findings from the Child and Adolescent Self-Harm in Europe (CASE) Study,' *Eur Child Adolesc Psychiatry,* vol.20, no.10, pp.498-508.

Madge N, Hewitt A, Hawton K, de Wilde E J, Corcoran P, Fekete S, van Heeringen K de Leo D and Ystgaard M, 2008, 'Deliberate self-harm within an international community sample of young people: comparative findings from the Child & Adolescent Self-harm in Europe (CASE) study,' *J Child Psychol Psychiatry,* vol.49, no.6, p.667-77.

McMahon M, O'Regan G, Corcoran P, Arensman E, Cannon M, Williamson E, Keeley H, 'Young Lives in Ireland: A school-based study of mental health and suicide prevention', 2017, National Research Foundation.

Melham N M, Day N, Shear M K, Day R, Reynolds C F, Brent D, 2004, 'Traumatic Grief Among Adolescents exposed to a peer's suicide,' *Am J Psychiatry,* vol.161, no.8, pp.1411-6.

Mental Health First Aid Australia, Revised 2016, 'Suicidal Thoughts and Safety Plans: Mental Health First Aid Guidelines',. (Online) Accessible: https://mhfa.com.au/sites/default/files/MHFA_suicide_guidelinesA4%202014%20Revised.pdf Sited: November 2018.

Michelson D. Bhugra D., 'Family environment, expressed emotion and adolescent self-harm: A review of conceptual, empirical, cross-cultural and clinical perspectives' *International Review of Psychiatry,* April 2012; volume 24, p 106–114.

Miguel E M, Chou T, Golik A, Cornacchino M S, Sanchez A, DeSerisy M, Comer J S, 'Examining the scope and patterns of deliberate self-injurious cutting content in popular social media', 2017, *Wiley Periodicals,* vol.34, pp.786–793.

Mission Australia, 2017, 'Youth Mental Health Report: Youth Survey 2012-2016,' Mission Australia and Black Dog Institute, Sydney.

Mission Australia, 2017, 'Youth Mental Health Report: Youth Survey 2012-2016,' Mission Australia and Black Dog Institute, Sydney.

Mitchell R, Seah R, Ting P H, Curtis K, Foster K, 2018, 'Intentional self-harm and assault hospitalisations and treatment cost of children in Australia over a ten year period', *Australian and New Zealand Journal of Public Health,* vol 42, pp.240-246.

Moreno M A, Ton A, Selkie E and Evans Y, 2016, 'Secret Society 123: Understanding the Language of Self-Harm on Instagram,' *J Adolesc Health,* vol.58, no.1, pp.78-84.

National Collaborating Centre for Mental Health, 2004, 'Self-harm: The short-term physical and psychological management and secondary prevention of self-harm in primary and secondary care', The British Psychological Society and The Royal College of Psychiatrists.

Nearchou F A, Bird N, Costello A, Duggan S, Gilroy J, Long R, McHugh L and Hennessy E, 2018 'Personal and perceived public mental-health stigma as predictors of help-seeking intentions in adolescents,' *J Adolesc,* vol.66, pp.83-90.

Nestler E J, Hyman S E and Malenka R, 2010, *Molecular Neuropharmacology,* New York: McGraw-Hill Medical.

Patchin J W and Hinduja S, 2017, 'Digital Self-Harm Among Adolescents,' *J Adolesc Health,* pp.761-6.

Psych Central, [Online]. Available: https://psychcentral.com/disorders/. (Accessed: October 2018)

Scoliers G, Portzyky G, Madge N, Hewitt A, Hawton K, de Wilde E J, Ystgaard M, Arensman E, De Leo D, Fekete S and van Heeringen K, 2008, 'Reasons for adolescent deliberate self-harm: A cry of pain and/or a cry for help? Findings from the child and adolescent self-harm in Europe (CASE) study,' *Soc Psychiatry Psychiatr Epidemiol,* vol.44, no.8, pp.601-7.

Someah K, 2012 'Common Self-Harm Behaviours', [Online]. Eating Disorder Hope, Available: https://www.eatingdisorderhope.com/treatment-for-eating-disorders/co-occurring-dual-diagnosis/self-injury/self-harm-as-a-co-occurring-issue-of-eating-disorders, (Accessed September 2018).

Stanley B, Sher L, Wilson S, Ekman R, Huang Y Y and Mann J J, 2010, 'Non-suicidal self-injurious behavior, endogenous opioids and monoamine neurotransmitters,' *J. Affect Disord.*, vol.224, no.1-2, pp.134-40.

The National Collaborating Centre for Mental Health, 2004, 'Self-harm: The short-term physical and psychological management and secondary prevention of self-harm in primary and secondary care', The British Psychological Society and The Royal College of Psychiatrists.

The National Suicidal Research Foundation, 2016, 'Northern Ireland Registry of Self-Harm: Regional Three-Year Report, 2012/13 to 2014/15', [Online] Available: http://www.publichealth.hscni.net/publications/northern-ireland-registry-self-harm-three-year-report-201213-201415 (Accessed October 2018)

The National Suicide Research Foundation, 'The National Self-Harm Registry Ireland,' [Online]. Available: https://www.nsrf.ie/our-research/our-systems/national-self-harm-registry-ireland/. (Accessed October 2018).

Townsend E, Wadman R, Sayal K, Armstrong M, Harroe C, Majumder P, Vostains P, Clarke D, 'Uncovering key patterns in self-harm in adolescents: Sequences analysis using the Card Sort

Task for Self-harm (CaTS)', 2016, *Journal of Affective Disorders,* Volume 206, pp.161–168.

Vivyan C, 'Get.gg,' 2011. [Online]. Available: https://www.getselfhelp.co.uk/docs/3Ds.pdf (Accessed Oct 10, 2018).

Weller C, 'A surprising number of teenagers are engaging in "digital self-harm,"' the practice of being mean to yourself online' [Online]. Business Insider Australia, Available: https://www.businessinsider.com.au/digital-self-harm-becoming-more-popular-among-teenagers-study-finds-2017-10?r=US&IR=T, [Accessed: Oct 10, 2018]

Wester K L, Trepal H C, 2017 'Non-Suicidal Self-Injury: Wellness Perspectives on Behaviours, Symptoms and Diagnosis', London and New York, Routledge Taylor and Francis Group.

Zetterqvist M, Svedin C G, Fredlund C, Priebe G, Wadsby M, Johnsson L S, 2018, 'Self-reported nonsuicidal self-injury (NSSI) and sex as a self-injury (SASI): Relationship to abuse, risk behaviors, trauma symptoms, self-esteem and attachment', Psychiatry Research, p.309–316.

Back Cover Material

If you have a child who is struggling with self-harm, I want to remind you that you are your child's greatest advantage. What you do and how you respond matters. This book was written for you and your family.—Michelle Mitchell

Self-harm is distressing and difficult for parents and caring adults to understand, as it seems to go against every instinct of self-protection and survival.

Author, educator and award-winning speaker Michelle Mitchell has over 20 years' experience working with and supporting children, parents and carers as they navigate this confronting mental health concern.

In this book she combines her experience with the latest research and interviews with experts and families to provide fresh insights into how to prevent, understand and respond to self-harm and digital self-harm.

Michelle answers questions like–

- Why does my child want to hurt themselves?
- What do I say if I suspect self-harm?
- How do I manage my child's safety?
- How do I take care of siblings and other family members?
- When should I seek support?

This unique resource will provide parents with the facts, practical help and comfort they need.

Michelle is an educator, author aid award-winning speaker whose passion is to support families, in 2000 Michelle left teaching and founded Youth Excel, a charity which supported thousands of young people with life skills education, mentoring and psychological services. Michelle's hands-on experience in the health and wellbeing sector have made her an engaging and sought after speaker. She lives in Brisbane, Australia with her husband and two teenagers.

www.ingramcontent.com/pod-product-compliance
Lightning Source LLC
Chambersburg PA
CBHW011747220426
43667CB00020B/2929